# Leadership Rules

What do great leaders need to do to run great schools? This exciting new book from Jo Facer takes the theory, ideas, and vision that so many leaders share and translates it into the small steps that busy school leaders can take that together lead to big positive changes.

Exploring the three cornerstones of a great education – behaviour, curriculum, and teaching – as well as the oft-neglected operations, the book outlines the theory and what best practice looks like in each area and then reveals the leadership actions that enable schools to get there. Each chapter also features real case studies from school leaders who explain how they have implemented the ideas and the impact they have had in their settings.

Full of practical, sustainable ideas to implement in the short and long term, this is essential reading for all leaders in primary and secondary schools.

**Jo Facer** is Head of the NPQ Faculty at the National Institute of Teaching, UK, and the author of *Simplicity Rules* (2019) and *Culture Rules* (2021), both published by Routledge.

# Leadership Rules

## What Leaders Need to Know and Do to Run Great Schools

Jo Facer

Routledge
Taylor & Francis Group

LONDON AND NEW YORK

First published 2025
by Routledge
4 Park Square, Milton Park, Abingdon, Oxon OX14 4RN

and by Routledge
605 Third Avenue, New York, NY 10158

*Routledge is an imprint of the Taylor & Francis Group, an informa business*

*British Library Cataloguing-in-Publication Data*
A catalogue record for this book is available from the British Library

*Library of Congress Cataloging-in-Publication Data*
Names: Facer, Jo, author.
Title: Leadership rules : what leaders need to know and do to run great
schools / Jo Facer.
Description: New York : Routledge, 2025. | Includes bibliographical
references.
Identifiers: LCCN 2024014251 (print) | LCCN 2024014252 (ebook) | ISBN
9781032736853 (hbk) | ISBN 9781032736846 (pbk) | ISBN 9781003465461
(ebk)
Subjects: LCSH: Educational leadership–Handbooks, manuals, etc. | School
management and organization–Handbooks, manuals, etc. | School
improvement programs–Handbooks, manuals, etc.
Classification: LCC LB2805 .F235 2025 (print) | LCC LB2805 (ebook) | DDC
371.2/011–dc23/eng/20240812
LC record available at https://lccn.loc.gov/2024014251
LC ebook record available at https://lccn.loc.gov/2024014252

ISBN: 978-1-032-73685-3 (hbk)
ISBN: 978-1-032-73684-6 (pbk)
ISBN: 978-1-003-46546-1 (ebk)

DOI: 10.4324/9781003465461

Typeset in Melior
by SPi Technologies India Pvt Ltd (Straive)

# Contents

# Acknowledgements

This book rests on the shoulders of school leaders who gave generously of their time to share their experiences. They are Matt Burnage, Tom Clements, Maria Craster, Sam Crome, Patrick Farmborough, Lindsay Galbraith, Josh Goodrich, Claire Hill, Abby Hughes, Becky Jones, James King, Stuart Morton, Tracey O'Brien, Rob Orme, Adam Rowe, Robbie Russell, David Thomas, Debbie Tremble, Hannah Turner, Tom Turnham, Dave Tushingham, Sarah Warnock, Claire White, and Chris White. In addition, I'd like to thank Jonathan Gower whose insights on Primary operations substantially improved Chapter 4.

Throughout writing this book, I drew on the wisdom of great teacher friends who lead their departments, schools, and Trusts with real integrity: Paul Bhatia, Elisabeth Bowling, Stuart Lock, Carly Moran, and Megan Reynard.

Finally, thank you to my colleagues at the National Institute of Teaching from whom I have learned so much over the past two years and who have helped to shape and sharpen my ideas about leadership in schools, particularly Natasha Brooks, Reuben Moore, Mariyam Mulla, Gene Payne, and Melanie Renowden.

# Introduction

What does great leadership mean? We are all, perhaps, familiar with the idea that great school leaders need strong domain knowledge, a compelling vision, an ability to lead others, and a good rapport with children and colleagues. But what do these sweeping statements really *mean*?

Take vision. I've read, and indeed I've said in my own writing, it is critical for school leaders to have thought carefully about their vision: what they want for their school community. While this is true, and I wouldn't advise leaders to avoid thinking about where they hope the children in their care will get to, the brutal reality is that most school visions boil down to be basically the same thing. With one or two notable exceptions, school visions essentially say: "to ensure our children do better than they would have otherwise done had they not come here, academically and non-academically." Even when you look for specialist provisions such as the Royal Ballet School, whose vision is "to be the best classical ballet school in the world," the ultimate meaning is to be brilliant at what we do for the children we serve. Nobody has a vision that says: "we will preserve the status quo, achieve average results, and the children will leave us with the same values and habits they arrived with." Everybody is in the job to improve things for young people.

The big question is this: what do we actually need to *do* as school leaders to make our schools great? How do we realise our vision, improving things for our young people? What is step 1? Step 2? And the thousand steps after that?

Which leads us to our second problem: implementation. While it is easy to find books which tell you what great curriculum, teaching, and behaviour should look like and how to get there, these aren't always translating into improved schools. I was once struck by seeing an individual delivering a session at a conference. It was completely inspiring – they had travelled to some of the top performing schools in this country and beyond, and they shared videos and information from those leaders and spoke knowledgeably about how those leaders had made schools which bucked the trend for disadvantaged young people and ensured they achieved results to rival or even surpass their more advantaged peers. This was a

DOI: 10.4324/9781003465461-1

professional who had seen great schools, worked with their leaders, and deeply engaged with the theory that sat behind all of that work.

But when I looked up the schools they led, I was struck by how very unlike the Charter schools they were. How, indeed, some were Ofsted (Office for Standards in Education, Children's Services and Skills)-inadequate. Some had progress 8 scores in the negative and multiple negatives for disadvantaged pupils.

I'm absolutely not denigrating this individual's work, which is why I'm not naming them and why I hope I've anonymised the example effectively here. They are a true expert, they work hard, they are committed to their community. So why can't they run great schools?

This is partly the pernicious knowing/doing gap. How often have you heard teachers run down their school's professional development session, complaining: "I already know all of that!," only to visit their classroom and see them... not doing it. We are all guilty of this. We know so much about education, but are we *doing* it? I've personally been plagued by my own inadequacies of doing for my entire career, and this book is my attempt to set out the "doing" stall for school leadership, at least partly to be better prepared myself for going back and leading some schools.

I think school leadership is one of the most complex topics in education, and the thing we need to get better at in it is knowing what to do at every stage of school improvement. In fine-grain detail. Part of the knowing/doing gap can be ameliorated by deepening our knowledge. Another part is about the deliberate practice of key things. A final part is knowing the micro-steps to take, when to take them, and what they need to look like.

And research is important – critically important. Research and theory of how children learn best, and how organisations best work, and how the curriculum is best structured underpin what is written here – sit behind it like a kind parent. But this is not a book about research. This is a book about what those armed with the research are doing step by step, day by day, to make some great practice in their school.

In this book, you will read about what to do to run a great school as a senior leader. We start with behaviour because without great behaviour, a great curriculum will not be learned no matter how well it is designed and delivered. First, the children need to be able to listen and follow instructions.

We move onto curriculum next, though, because what you choose to teach and why matter. The third chapter will explore teaching and particularly the development of teachers – the aspect within our control which is most likely to lead to improved outcomes for young people.[1]

The final chapter is a compendium of "the other stuff": often brutally ignored but absolutely crucial: the operational aspects of running of a school that senior leaders need to get right for the school to work well.

Throughout this book, I lean on more expert colleagues to help to exemplify aspects of great school leadership. This book rests on the shoulders of those giants.

There are pockets of greatness all over our country, where school leaders are doing the things that will create the conditions for all children to flourish, and I hope that I will render these in enough detail that we can hope to understand and perhaps emulate their work.

Ultimately, as erstwhile Headteacher Gene Payne is fond of reminding me, "what we do eats what we know for breakfast." It is not our ideas or knowledge but our everyday actions that create the schools we run. This book attempts to set out what those actions might be.

## Note

1 Education Endowment Foundation (2021). Effective Professional Development: Guidance Report.

# 1 Behaviour

For school leaders, and particularly leaders of behaviour, whole-school routines become a priority. They are the visible vantage point of a school's behaviour and culture and the easiest (though not necessarily the most accurate) way of seeing, at a glance, how strong the behaviour and culture are in a school. For pastoral leaders, they can become an obsession and a measure. While leaders seek to move from a consequences-driven school to one that is more culture-driven, dismissing routines is a risky route to achieving this.

Shared routines are critical to creating safe and welcoming school environments. It is in moments when a whole school moves – in secondary schools, this can mean upwards of a thousand young people – that pupils are most vulnerable to incidents. This is why colleagues of mine report children being "afraid" of corridors, of one colleague's maternity risk assessment noting she should not be in the school corridors during lesson changeover, and why at one fire drill at a school I taught in two girls flew at each other, screaming – the kind of incident that in a less controlled school could have started a pile-on but thankfully was isolated and swiftly dealt with by leaders.

When we bring all our school community together, we see, for better or worse, what the culture is of our setting.

In this chapter, we'll briefly look at the Education Endowment Foundation's (EEF's) implementation theory through the lens of introducing whole-school routines, before considering the specifics of practice, thinking about entry and exit to school, line-ups, assemblies, lunch time, and moving between lessons. We'll also hear from some school leaders about how they would go about orchestrating changes and improvements to their school's routines.

DOI: 10.4324/9781003465461-2

# The EEF's guide to implementation

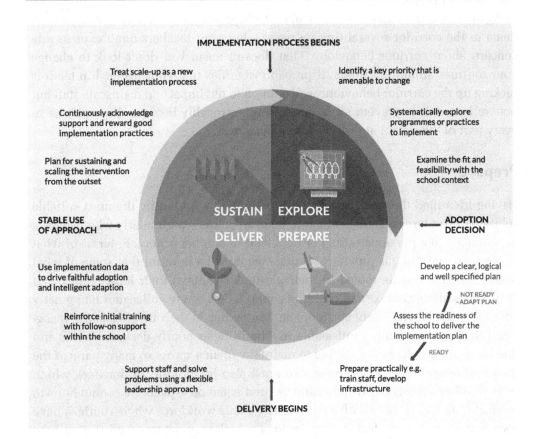

**IMPLEMENTATION PROCESS BEGINS**

Treat scale-up as a new
implementation process

Identify a key priority that is
amenable to change

Continuously acknowledge
support and reward good
implementation practices

Systematically explore
programmes or practices
to implement

Plan for sustaining and
scaling the intervention
from the outset

Examine the fit and
feasibility with the
school context

**STABLE USE
OF APPROACH**

SUSTAIN EXPLORE

DELIVER PREPARE

**ADOPTION
DECISION**

Use implementation data
to drive faithful adoption
and intelligent adaption

Develop a clear, logical
and well specified plan

NOT READY
- ADAPT PLAN

Reinforce initial training
with follow-on support
within the school

Assess the readiness of
the school to deliver the
implementation plan

READY

Support staff and solve
problems using a flexible
leadership approach

Prepare practically e.g.
train staff, develop
infrastructure

**DELIVERY BEGINS**

## Explore

One of the most striking aspects of the EEF's implementation guidance[1] is the amount of energy and time prior to delivery. Fifty per cent of this cycle occurs before roll-out, and while that might seem unrealistic to school leaders, accustomed as schools are to taking swift action when they see things are not as they should be, we will probably all confess that rolling out a new initiative probably would have gone better if we had gone more slowly.

I think there is a balance to be struck: as in all application of the best evidence, it has to work for your school and your context. That's why when we hear from some school leaders who have been successful in implementing new practices, you'll want to pay attention to exactly how long they spent tee-ing up changes.

Prior to introducing a change to a whole-school routine, you need to **identify** what the aspect is that needs to change: what's the problem?

In one school I worked in, this was done through an annual staff survey. The Headteacher combed through the survey meticulously, searching especially for themes and common areas of challenge for colleagues. The benefit of gathering many voices is that you are then genuinely sure this is a concern for colleagues and not just a pet project.

Again, there is a balance to be struck. Perhaps you, as a leader, deal with incidents in the corridor several times a week – but your teachers don't express any concern about corridor behaviour. That doesn't mean you don't look to change your routines around corridors; it probably signifies that your leadership team is picking up the corridor behaviour well enough to not impact on mainscale staff but not well enough to prevent all issues arising – probably because they can't be in every part of the school at every lesson changeover.

## Prepare

Having identified the issue at stake, leaders must then identify the most suitable solution. It can be easy here to revert to what we know – particularly what we have experienced in a previous setting or on a visit to another school. In terms of what we've seen work in our previous schools, we must be mindful that some of what makes schools work is rooted in their particular context: their local context but also their staffing context and building context. One of my colleagues had greatly admired schools with silent corridors but, on taking on their first headship, recognised that this was simply unfeasible in a building as poorly designed as his and that he would not have the staffing to maintain silence across so many parts of the school at every lesson changeover. We must also be mindful of practices which work in other schools but which could be predicated on aspects we cannot hope to replicate, such as schools with a particularly stable workforce where routines have been embedded and perfected over decades, which may not translate so readily to one where 30% of staff were new in September, for example.

When we're sure we've got the right issue and the right solution for our particular context, there is, according to the EEF, still work to be done before we roll this out. As a former school leader, I find that this is the point the EEF has me pulling out my hair – I've got my solution now; we need to do it right away! I don't have time for more of this groundwork-laying, I've got children to make a better school for!

This is partly based on my experience of working in schools where changes were implemented with astonishing rapidity. I've worked in different contexts – a new start school, where the small, aligned, and exceptional staff team would make major changes from day to day that felt streamlined for pupils and managed to stick; a large London academy where the systems and processes were so well embedded that changing one thing felt manageable and was swiftly done – but it is true that this won't be the case in all settings, and indeed I've also been the frustrated staff member who has watched initiatives launched to great acclaim, only to be forgotten weeks later. I think one of the signs you've not implemented well as a senior leader is when a colleague says something like "are we still asking them to take their coats off in the corridors?"

So as much as it can feel like the EEF doesn't *get* the pace of schools, I think we can all admit that there are times we could have gone slower and had more impact in the long run.

So, before you roll out your initiative, there is still some deep preparing to do. First, you're going to ensure that your school environment is ready for this change. Is it the run-up to SATs, and all your year 6 teachers are feeling stressed and run off their feet? Or is it off the back of a scary lunchtime fight, and your team is desperate for a change and excited to implement it now?

When your environment feels ready, now is the time to train the team. What might this look like? The obvious start is with professional development, and a single session of input is not the way to make training stick – have a look forward to Chapter 3 if you want more on this now. Whatever your setup, and we'll look at some great examples of effective Continuing Professional Development (CPD) later, you'll need to talk to colleagues about what is changing and give them some training in it. You'll want to make sure they have an opportunity to practice it – ideally, by standing up and doing it. That's often, with routines, where you can see how well you've communicated your language. I remember implementing "STAR" (a shortcut to asking pupils to put their pens down, sit up straight, and look to the front of the room) at one school and hearing a colleague say: "3-2-1 and STAR-ing me in 3-2-1 and STAR" – not quite the quick, simple message we'd hoped for.

After teachers are trained, the next critical aspect of sharing the message with pupils is on our list. When communicating a whole-school routine change or even when reminding pupils of key routines either at the start of a new term or when a routine is going awry, there are plenty of options: through assemblies, tutor time, leaders popping into classrooms, letters home, and so on. As a rule of thumb, the bigger the change, the fewer the voices. For a new approach to line-up, have the same Vice Principal lead the same assembly on the same day to every year group, with all teachers attending at least one. This makes the message cleaner and clearer for all.

Just as you'll read with adults and professional development, ensure that pupils can practice the routine. If they're lining up, get them into the space they will do it, and practice it. Take as long as is needed to reach the standard you want to set for the long term – remember that time invested in teaching routines will reap additional learning time when the routines are practised and slick.

## Sustain

The EEF is upfront about letting us know that change is hard and that to anticipate immediate perfection is folly. There will be teething difficulties in any new routine, and teachers and leaders should feel ready for this and not disheartened when they occur. I've worked in too many settings where a good idea was thrown out after a week because it wasn't great (yet), leading to yet more turbulent change and confusion with staff and pupils. Stick with it, encourage teachers to bring issues to you, and seek to resolve them together. Be ready to invest as much time in following up and checking that teachers understand and feel confident with the new routine as you did in the initial, start-up phase.

## Back to routines, then

Great routines are the backbone of great schools. A helpful bar for your routines is articulated by Sam Strickland, who says: "if your behaviour systems do not allow the most inexperienced member of staff the platform to teach without their lessons being interrupted or hijacked by behaviour, then your systems are not as robust as you think."[2] Whole-school routines are a signal to the community that "this is how we do things here." They are the most visible sign of compliance the school community – staff and pupils – have, and a great bellwether for how bought-in pupils and staff are to what the school is doing. Even more important than culture and buy-in, though, is that these routines ensure the safe and calm movement of the entire school community. Any time many hundreds of individuals move in a small space, there is the potential for harm – either accidental (think: tripping up, bumping into one another) or intended (think: no one will see what I do to this person in this area, and I don't like them so I'm going to do something unkind). Great whole-school routines keep children safe.

## Entry and exit to school

The start of the school day, any school day, is carefully thought out in the best schools. There is a time the gates open, and that time is communicated to parents and carers and children clearly. Someone is responsible for unlocking those gates – sometimes the school caretaker, sometimes a rotating member of staff, sometimes the Headteacher themselves.

On allowing pupils into school, someone should be there at the gate to greet them, and someone should be in the receiving area – playground, school hall, classrooms – ready to receive them and ensure their safety and wellbeing in that place. The gate is a great place to get it right at the start of the day, and in a large school (or with particularly large gates where many children can come in all at once), it could require multiple members of staff.

At the gate, look for uniform – the easiest, most visible sign of compliance. Where uniform is still not secured, you will definitely want more than one person on the gate, as every time you stop a child to fix their shirt or tie or have a discussion about nail polish, you stop the flow of children into the building. If this causes a back-up onto the street, this becomes unsafe for children and pedestrians in the local area.

As well as compliance, warmth is critical. I once heard an inspiring Deputy Head say: "the most important thing I do is greet every child, every morning." Working in a new-start school, she knew every child's name. Certainly, use their name if you know it. For children, their name is often their most prized possession, and it is a signal that they are seen and known. It contributes to their feeling safe, secure, and welcome in school.

Leaders think carefully about the staffing of the mornings. While you have to balance the wellbeing and needs of staff with pupils (the morning is normally precious time to finish photocopying and setting up for the day, and school days begin early enough as it is, making it tough for teachers, especially those with caring responsibilities at home, to get in early enough to have a smooth start), someone should be on the playground or in the area to circulate and check that pupils have started the day calmly. In my experience, the mornings are the calmest time of the day, with the exception of the start of term when the energy and noise are normally positive excitement.

At the end of the day, pupils need a signal that they are seen before they enter the local community. At one school I worked in, we'd remind pupils of uniform expectations where they weren't being met, noting they represented the school whenever they wore the uniform. I've also found that "see you tomorrow!" is an important phrase to say cheerily as often as possible, ideally targeting pupils whose attendance isn't the best. And, of course, if you've seen or heard about anything brilliant happening, make sure you briefly mention it: "star writing in period 2 today, well done Alesha!" That said, children are always keen to return home or to their friends (or, depressingly, to their phones), so some probably won't appreciate a lengthy speech at this point on their achievements.

In primary schools, the gate becomes a crucial space where parents and teachers can meet, and primary colleagues will very often follow classes out and catch parents for a quick word in person. This is an excellent opportunity to catch issues before they become concerns and to build the relationship so home and school can work more effectively in partnership together.

## Line-ups

Line-ups are more often used in secondary schools as a formal moment, prior to learning beginning, where children line up in their form or teaching groups, normally in a large space outside, before transitioning silently into the school building. I've seen these done wonderfully in a number of primary schools, although they tend to be faster to move out of the playground and often not quite silent.

It is very easy to get line-ups wrong. At one school I visited, I noted the pupils went from playing to lining up, hearing a motivational message from a Head of Year (HoY), and entering the building in under 3 minutes. I turned to my host, a Vice Principal, in wonder; she, on the other hand, was grimacing: "it needs to be quicker."

The best leaders keep raising the bar. For that leader, three minutes was too long spent not learning. When I visited the school again a few years later, I noticed they had installed giant outdoor clocks, so it was clear to pupils and staff what the time was. This created an impressive visual signal that their time mattered.

However, for leaders looking to introduce line-ups, do not be dismayed when your early attempts clock in at well over three minutes. Lining up and entering their building, if new to pupils, will take time to get right. It is better to invest the time to get pupils silent and walking in silently in their lines, rather than allowing them to chat – eventually, chatting pupils entering the building in a clump will take longer than a silent straight line.

I've always felt that line-ups are a great time for the HoY or a member of senior staff to address the year group, though some colleagues prefer to save that precious 30 seconds to a minute for learning and enter the building faster. If you do have someone address pupils, have it be swift – under a minute – and almost always positive. Reminders of the importance of learning and the year group's prior success at it work well. Occasionally, if the year group has got something really wrong, there is no reason they can't be told about it – but the positive should outweigh the negative by a significant factor, or they will lose their buy-in to the line-up.

---

### Rob Orme, Vice Principal at Ark Soane Academy, shares his approach to leading line-ups

*At Ark Soane Academy, we are intentional about how each moment of the day runs. Nothing is left to chance. We want the school to be a joyful, safe, and orderly place where things are done in a calm and efficient way. We also want there to be a predictability to how things are done that makes it easy for students to do the right thing. We use routines to achieve these goals.*

*An example is line-up. At the start of day, after morning break and after lunch, hundreds of students need to move through very limited space at the same time to get to their classrooms. In challenging schools, the loudest, worst-behaved students can take advantage of these moments and take charge of determining culture. Unkindness, pushing, and boisterousness become rife. Students arrive to lessons across a five (or more)-minute period, 'traffic on the stairs miss'. Worse, they disappear to the toilets to truant. Particularly for younger, quieter, or less confident students, these moments of the day can feel unsafe. Incidents from outside lessons trickle into them, and precious learning time is wasted. Our solution is line-up.*

*Each year group has an area where they line up alphabetically in classes. There is a raised platform at the front for the Head of Year to stand. When the Head of Year blows a whistle, students have 60 seconds to stand with one foot either side of lines painted at 1.5 metre intervals on the ground. Painting lines may sound excessive, but like all routines, success lies in the detail. When lines are too close together, there is more opportunity for misbehaviour, it is harder for students to move to them and harder for teachers to walk and scan their line. Painted lines also remove the need for teachers nagging for students to stand in a straighter line which can be met by students publicly ignoring the instruction, which undermines the teacher. Instead, teachers can focus on cheerily greeting students and checking the uniform is smart.*

*After 60 seconds, the Head of Year raises their hand to signify silence. All staff and students do the same before lowering hands. The Head of Year then delivers a brief, motivational pep talk. The aim of this is to build positive year group identity and a sense of unity by celebrating students demonstrating the school's values and encouraging all students to be their best. It means the Head of Year sets the culture ahead of lessons, rather than the worst-behaved students. It allows everybody to move purposefully and calmly to lessons ready to focus.*

*The success of line-up hinges on attention to detail, training for staff and students, and ongoing monitoring. For every routine, we write down exactly what should happen, so that the expected standard is clear and potential difficulties can be worked through by Senior Leadership Team (SLT) ahead of training staff and students. This codification also ensures that the rationale and practicalities do not live in the head of one person who may at any time leave the school – the routine can outlive their tenure.*

*Staff training focuses on why, what, and then practicing how. For line-up, this means explaining why we do line-up, the consequences of a staff member not doing their role, how to organise a line, what to look for, what to say, how to stand, and so on. In their first days at the school, students also practice until they have mastered how to do it. As with all routines, this time invested finessing it at the outset pays dividends.*

*Like any routine, standards slide without vigilance. If everybody is doing and nobody is watching, it is hard to have a sense of standards. For this reason, there is a member of SLT assigned to each year group line-up each day. They support as needed, but their primary role is to observe what is happening and make sure we are doing what we say we are doing. They also provide feedback to the Head of Year and teachers, send a polite reminder to any staff arriving late to lines and feedback to SLT if staff training is needed. Where improvements can be made to any routine or the whole-school routine starts to feel like a weak point in the school day, it becomes the school focus of the week, discussed in staff meetings and emailed out as a reminder in our daily all staff email until it is up to standard again.*

## Assemblies

In the school I attended, and in the first school I worked in, we had whole-school assemblies. In the school I attended, a tiny rural private school (accessed through an almost 100% funded government-assisted place), year groups contained 40 pupils, and the secondary phase started from year 9. Entering assembly was rapid (or at least it felt fast). Conversely, in the 120 published admission numbers (PAN) secondary school I first worked in, getting year 7 to 13 into the hall took upwards of ten minutes, as did getting the pupils out.

Assemblies are a logistical nightmare. If you're spending 20 minutes getting in and out and ten minutes talking to the group about something of value, it needs to be worthy of the 30 minutes of time invested.

Most large secondary schools I have worked in since then held year group assemblies, or House assemblies, instead of whole-school assemblies. Then I missed the sense of coming together as a school community – there is something incredibly special about the whole school being in one room regularly, and having nearly 800 people in one room signals a strong culture. Leaders need to make the call on who comes together, how often, and for how long.

In one school I worked in, the assembly hall was accessed directly from the playground through two sets of double doors. Pupils could "fill up" from the front and back, and entry took less than five minutes. But the hall was small, so only one year group at a time could have an assembly. Your building will give you some constraints, and you'll need to work out the best way for you to use pupil time to instil culture.

It is very hard to behaviour-manage an assembly. One astounding Head I know became the Executive Head of a very challenging local school. I remember her telling the story of how at her first assembly at that school, she told the pupils she expected silence for assemblies, she knew they were capable of that, and she'd wait for them to be silent. The first assembly it took 20 minutes, but they got there. The next assembly, she waited barely five minutes. After that, they knew she meant business. They came in, largely, without talking.

As enormous as the mountain seems to climb in schools that are chaotic, it's reassuring to remember that children are children, they are able to do all kinds of things (more amazing than sitting in silence!) – and you have to believe and share your belief that they will get there.

## Transitions between lessons

There is a growing popularity of silent transitions between lessons. The education world often feels divided between those who want to minimise disruption and maximise minutes of learning at all costs and those who feel that school is also a time for pupils to practise self-regulation and that a few minutes added on is a small price to pay for pupils enjoying trust and freedom. Along with philosophy, school context will need to play a part in how far down the spectrum of minimal supervision to total silence you feel you need to go. By school context, I mean both the physical space you have and the staff available and the current behaviour of pupils in corridors.

Where corridors are exceptionally noisy or unsafe and where pupils regularly arrive more than five minutes late to a lesson, I would urge leaders to consider investing, at least for the short term, in staffing corridors to bring them to a calmer, happier state. One of my most dreadful memories of being a deputy head was working with the family of a boy who had received a very serious sanction, who claimed he had not attacked another boy in the corridor. As part of the meeting, they requested the CCTV footage, which we viewed together with a police officer (leaders will know just how contentious exclusions can be). They requested to see the footage over and over, and it was heartbreaking. No child should fear being attacked in their school.

Where staffing and your building are an issue, I would advise against creating a rod for your own back. If you ask for silence but you cannot staff it, the pupils could get the message that you do not mean what you say. The only solution I have found to this kind of problem is to train teachers to dismiss their class on time and stand at the door while they dismiss them – one foot in, one foot out, as it were. The mere presence of staff ought to dissuade pupils from any serious or extreme behaviours. With training and with explanations for pupils, and with every member of SLT out of their office and positioned to cover as much of the school as they can (perhaps walking through corridors at a set route to gain coverage), you can usually bring corridors under control and manage quiet, if not silent, corridors.

If your building and staffing allow, silent corridors are an option you might consider. In the schools I have worked in and with that use this method, care is taken for staff to be trained in how to manage their pupils during transitions, and this is often rehearsed at the start of every full term, even years into functioning, to continue to raise the standard (which here usually means: remember what silence means; move more quickly). Silent corridors ensure that pupils get to their lessons quickly and safely, and it is by far the most efficient method, if not the most popular with staff who, in my experience, need to be perennially on duty to make this magic happen. Silent corridors can feel strange for pupils, and some educationalists may fear they feel oppressive (not in my experience, but I've not visited all schools with silent corridors), so in the best schools care is taken to train teachers to maximise their positive interactions on this transition, such as by greeting pupils by name or praising them for their speed and silence.

On arriving at their next lesson, do pupils enter the classroom or line up outside? Again, your building will need to dictate this to some extent – it simply may not be possible to line up outside some (or any) rooms. A benefit of entering straightaway means no learning time is lost; a drawback is that you then have pupils in the room for different lengths of time, so teachers will need to have a task on the board pupils can get on with – which is hard to meaningfully plan, given some will do it for 3 minutes and others for 3 seconds. I would urge leaders who assume that more time in class at any cost is better to carefully consider the guidance any teacher will need to get a really good "do now" task planned for every lesson in these circumstances.

---

### Rob Orme, Vice Principal at Ark Soane Academy, shares his insights on managing corridors

*Before students enter the building for lessons, they line up. When students move from line-up to lessons, they walk swiftly (keeping up with the person in front) and in single file with eyes forward. The width of the staircase*

> *means two classes can enter at once, so students walk in double-file, which speeds up entry. Staff who aren't teaching that period are allocated a duty point along the route to ensure there are no blind spots. Our corridors are not silent. They are orderly and efficient but joyfully noisy as students greet each adult they pass with eye contact and a cheery 'good morning sir/miss.' Politeness rings out across the school, a reminder that we are one community and we behave in a calm and kind way. Lessons start crisply and purposefully with all students arriving at the same time. The possibility of internal truancy is removed.*

## Lunch time

The continuum of managing lunch runs, in my experience, from a fully staffed, fully choreographed family lunch experience, to a grab-and-go free-for-all. Everything works somewhere, and nothing works everywhere. When you're considering the best way to manage lunch, you will need to carefully consider your context. How many pupils fit in the dining area? How many serveries can you open? How much time do you have for lunch break? How fast can your canteen staff serve pupils?

Most schools do not allow pupils to enter the dining hall when they choose. This is because most schools do not have the luxury of space, and to have no routine would lead to immense queues over lunch. I've worked in schools where the "order" of pupils varied from week to week, which feels complex to me but which was explained once to pupils and seemed to work well, probably because if a year group is told: "when you hear three pips, that is year 9's signal to enter the dining hall," very hungry teenagers are motivated to remember this. They will also benefit from the peer effect whereby they see lots of their friends moving towards lunch, so they go as well.

Family lunch can be a really beautiful event, and there is something special about having your place to sit, especially as a teenager when social anxiety is high anyway. Having teachers eat with pupils does wonders to improve relationships. That said, it is a massive time investment as well as financial: providing lunch for every member of staff every day of the year is a small fortune, and if pupils know lunch will be given to them whether they pay or not, you would be surprised (or not) how many families do not pay. (In one school I knew well, as few as a quarter of all parents paid, leaving the other three quarters dining for free – and that excludes any pupil eligible for free school meals. After an intense communication campaign to chase the families who weren't eligible for free school meals but were not paying did not make up the numbers, the school had to choose between discontinuing family dining or hiking the price for the families who were paying; it chose the former.)

In one school I worked at, space was at a premium. When pupils could choose their seating, lunch was running over by 20 minutes most days. Pupils were saving places for their friends, then waiting for their friends to finish their food. Arguments broke out over who could sit where, and the most vulnerable pupils were afraid to go into the canteen. The school decided to introduce a more structured approach, where pupils had to sit in the next available seat. Although some educators would feel uncomfortable with not allowing pupils free choice, this solved a number of issues, not least that of the anxiety of pupils not knowing where to sit, it enabled pupils to make new connections, and it meant lunch ran to time every day.

However you manage lunch, if you manage lunch, it will require staff to be on duty, and we will look into duties more in Chapter 4.

Whole-school routines are important, but if you ask any teacher, they will probably not name these as the most important aspect of pupil behaviour. That is because most teachers care far more about what happens in their classroom than in the whole school. Indeed, I knew of one very large secondary that had perfect line-ups in pin-drop silence and massive issues of behaviour in the majority of classrooms. In some ways, leaders can control whole-school set-piece events by having a strong presence and fixing some issues themselves – it is far harder to control what happens inside individual classrooms, and so that is where we turn our attention now.

## Classroom routines

Your own philosophy and school context will determine to what extent you choose to mandate any classroom routines. Again, schools are on a continuum from low to high autonomy. There are benefits to allowing teachers to be autonomous in how they conduct their classes, and certainly some pupil contexts are amenable to this, but in my experience, a level of consistency in the routines that teachers use across a school supports pupils to feel that their classroom experiences are safe and predictable. At the same time, I've heard horror stories (unproven and widely disputed) of certain trusts that expect "all teachers to be on the same slide in the same lesson." Mandating every move a teacher makes is likely to devalue colleagues and make them feel untrusted. Any whole-school routine you want teachers to embed in their classrooms must be clearly communicated: why this routine and not another? What are the benefits to pupils of all teachers using this same routine?

We'll now look at some of the most common whole-school classroom routines. This isn't intended to be a book about how to do them – for that, I'd recommend Doug Lemov's *Teach Like a Champion 3.0*, my go-to book for how to do anything brilliantly in a classroom setting. Here, we're looking at how leaders might select routines and why.

## Getting the class's attention

"3-2-1, and SLANT"; "1-2-3, eyes on me"; a series of claps; "hands on top – that means stop"; a hand raised. There are almost endless ways teachers call a class to attention. In my early years of teaching, I tried to save my poor tired voice by using a hotel bell bought with the best of intentions from Amazon. More than once, a pupil snuck this from my desk and would randomly start dinging it through the lesson. Eventually, the bell went missing – I have a fairly good idea which past pupil has it, and I hope it is enjoying its new home. Safe to say, the bell was not a winner.

Desperate teachers will try quite a lot to get their class to stop talking and start looking at the front. It is the job of leaders to make it as easy as possible for teachers to call their class to attention. A benefit of having one way of doing this is that pupils get a lot of practice – every teacher using the routine four or five or 10 times in a lesson means pupils know what to expect, and you won't have the nightmare scenario I was warned about in teacher training, of a trainee standing at the front of a rowdy class with her hand in the air, as a well-meaning student asked her if she had a question she wanted to ask.

I've seen schools use a silent signal brilliantly. A hand up might be missed, but if every other pupil puts their hand in the air and stops speaking, you've got a go-to signal that works in classrooms as well as in your largest, most disparate situations, including the physical education (PE) fields and a school trip. On the other hand, a benefit of using a countdown, such as "321 and," is that pupils have a run-up to compliance, perhaps making it more likely they will be silent and comply first time. A benefit of an acronym like "SLANT" or "STAR"[3] is that this can reinforce some of your key school values, and re-teaching it to pupils becomes about not just compliance but a whole attitude to learning.

## Entering the classroom

Less frequent than requiring attention, this is still something that every teacher does multiple times a day. Do pupils enter the classroom silently, or can they quietly talk? Do they stand behind chairs or sit straight down? Do they take their books out or await your instructions? Do they read until the lesson starts?

As with all routines, having one way of coming into the room can support pupils feeling safe and welcome in their environment. The last thing you want is a pupil sitting down, happily beginning their work and being reprimanded for this because, unlike the lesson before, *this* teacher likes them to stand behind their chairs.

I'm a fan of silent entries – the gentle murmuring of the earliest four children can quickly escalate with a full class – and routines which ensure that everyone is ready to start. My personal preference is lining up outside or standing behind chairs, because I like everyone to benefit from the recap starter activities I favour and have written about in *Simplicity Rules*, but I have seen phenomenal schools where pupils enter, sit down, and learn straightaway. Both ways can work well, but I also believe both ways work best when everyone in the school does the same thing.

## Handing out

Teachers seem to be perennially handing out: books, exercise books, worksheets, homework – the list is endless. Though behaviour management experts will recommend that you allow your trickiest customer to hand out books as an opportunity for praise, this can backfire as well. (I've had books of pupils "go missing," marking a tragic start to the class for sometimes emotional year 7 pupils in particular.) Even the most willing and lovely pupils will guilelessly ask: "who's Tommy?" leaving poor Tommy feeling unseen.

Even pupils who know everyone's name will tend to hand out books inexcusably slowly, holding up the start of the lesson. The only class I've enlisted their support to hand out books was one where pupils were coming from all corners of school from their GCSE (General Certificate of Secondary Education) options, so the start of the lesson was always delayed by a number of minutes.

Otherwise, I'd advocate the teacher handing out. Ideally, arrange your class in long rows and stack books on the end of the row. Then pupils can simply hand the books or worksheets down. You might make a game of this so pupils in the different rows compete to be fastest at this. As with all routines, never assume that telling pupils how to do this once will suffice. Support teachers to troubleshoot, so they're ready to pre-empt with pupils what happens if a book is in the wrong row or what happens if overenthusiastic pupils end up dropping books on the floor (especially a hazard with your keenest to win; think KS3 and upper KS2).

This routine is a great timesaver, and if every teacher in every classroom uses the same method for handing out materials, pupils will reap the rewards of many saved minutes and hours over the course of a school year.

## Answering questions

While you aren't likely to want to script every classroom routine for teachers, another way to make life easier for staff and more predictable for pupils is a routine around answering questions. All teachers in all lessons are likely to ask pupils questions, and in the best, most dynamic lessons, this will feel almost constant during explanations and recaps. I've seen wonderful schools where pupils don't raise their hands and instead offer their contributions as they think of them, admittedly in some fairly affluent areas. This can absolutely work in some contexts, although I'd advise leaders in schools like this to dig into whether there are any pupils who are *not* offering their thoughts or answering questions in these schools. Where pupils self-direct their offerings, a space opens up for them to sit quietly disengaged.

In most schools I've worked in, this would not work – pupils are either too enthusiastic or too little self-regulated to be able to turn-take calmly. For those reading who think pupils will need to learn this to succeed as adults, I'll say that most adults do not find themselves in 30-person meetings, and those who do tend to find that either a few voices dominate or hand-raising becomes a norm. Indeed, I've noticed that in online meetings of over five people, hand-raising becomes the default to avoid chaos. Your context determines what is needed, and I would argue that classrooms benefit from hands up to ensure equity of opportunity and to promote calm environments. Something as simple as ensuring that pupils raise their hands to contribute should be, in most schools, set as a clear expectation with teachers and pupils. With very small sixth form groups, this may not be needed – again, your context will dictate how widespread this routine needs to be across your school.

Some schools dispense with "hands up" questioning altogether, preferring that teachers "cold call" pupils. The benefit of this system is it has the teacher fully in control and able to drive who is called on in each lesson, ensuring (we would hope) a good spread of voices and engagement from the whole class. If you wish to do this, you will want to train staff and pupils with the "why" and "how" of this technique, as children in secondary school will have spent many years putting their hands up, and it will be a challenge for them to stop this, as well as frustrating for your more bought-in, keener pupils.

Personally, I've always liked a mixture of hands-up and hands-down questioning, but this mix starts to lead us to teaching and learning techniques, which is not the topic of this chapter. Suffice to end this by saying: decide on an approach and communicate it to everyone and then check it is happening.

## Leaving the classroom

The final aspect of classroom behaviour you might want to implement a whole-school routine for is how pupils leave the classroom. Particularly if you use bells to signal the end of a lesson and particularly when lessons are before break and lunch, pupils are keen to move, and having an uncontrolled end to a lesson can leave the room in a way that leads to teachers needing to work hard to put it together. In some schools, particularly those with easily crowded corridors, pupils leaving calmly can be beneficial for whole-school calmness – rather than a rowdy mob flooding into a small space, which could potentially lead to harm.

I've worked in schools with a 1-2-3 routine, where teachers use a silent signal to mark which part of the routine they'd like, and pupils comply; so (1) they might pack their things away, (2) they might stand behind their chairs, and (3) they might leave. If this works well, great! I have found this to overcomplicate things, as judged by the number of times I saw teachers ignoring this routine or getting it wrong, and supply teachers who never knew this.

In terms of finishing calmly, I'm not sure you need anything more complicated than asking pupils to stand behind their chairs in silence, and then dismissing them a row at a time. This has the added benefit of speeding everyone up, as you can dismiss the row ready first, for example. If you have compliant, quick pupils, this is a lovely opportunity to call out great effort: "Eniola, you worked really hard today and wrote a great paragraph – your row can lead out."

If you have a bell and teachers reach readiness in advance, a habit that is good to instil is asking pupils recap questions orally for the last few minutes. Depending on the age and ability of the group, they will be more willing or completely unwilling to engage at this point in the lesson, so I'd advise teachers to use cold call for the majority of this short period. Asking oral questions right to the bell demonstrates that you value every minute of learning and that you aren't interested in routines for the sake of routines.

There may be other routines for the classroom and whole school that are important to you as a leader to get right. Only you know your school context: if you feel you need more consistency in key areas of learning, introduce those routines. If you feel your teachers can hold more in their heads and get it to the level you desire, introduce those routines. And if your school is a well-oiled machine and you have more routines, keep those routines! This is meant to guide leaders who are considering what to implement in schools that are at a different stage of their journeys.

---

### James King, Headteacher at Park House School, shares his insights on how to improve routines across a school

*With the school in special measures, behaviour a '4' and previously been focussed on restorative practice, I spent a period of time reviewing the behaviour policies of all the secondary schools in the Trust and then visited a number of these schools to see these policies being applied. I designed our policy, a hybrid of the preferred parts of each school, to be context specific and to elicit rapid improvements in behaviour.*

*I talked it over with my line manager and walked through how key elements would work practically in an attempt to eliminate any potential snags. Key areas of focus were student entry to school, morning roll call, classroom expectations and how we would send students to the referral room.*

*I spent time reviewing systems, looking for loopholes and ensuring that systems were clear and procedurally 'watertight': the 'what if's' were ironed out prior to launch.*

*"Win the morning, win the day" was a mantra we held dear, and to get this part right, we repeatedly modelled, explained and practised roll call as year groups, as key stages and then the whole school, before it was rolled out "properly." To ensure the start of the day was calm and well managed, it was essential to limit student movement around school. We therefore decided on one entry point and having each year group with their own location to gather in, which made supervision more straightforward.*

*Expectations for uniform and equipment were over communicated to parents and students and support was offered for those where we foresaw challenges. Similarly, we over-communicated our revised behavioural expectations to parents and students. We held assemblies and parents' meetings to detail exactly what was expected and the rationale that sat behind – the what and the why.*

*The underlying message was to ensure students had the best chance of success in a disruption free environment. It was what they deserved and what we committed to providing.*

*Simplicity and consistency were key: any student failing to follow the expectations would have their name put on the board. A further failing led to a referral to our referral room. We opted away from SLT 'on call' collecting students and instead put the onus on students to get there promptly themselves. If a student failed to arrive within 5 minutes, they would be suspended and their time in referral completed on their return. To enable this, we developed (with the help of some excellent IT technicians) a piece of software called 'quick contacts' that all staff had on their desktop and when a student was sent, it updated 'live' the dashboard in the referral room and was available to all SLT and Heads of Year. It provided a countdown for the time to arrive to the referral room – we allowed 5 minutes, as it was possible to get there from anywhere in the school within 5 minutes.*

*This represented a significant change from previous practice in the school, and supporting staff to buy in and use these new systems would be critical to their success. Staff had previously worked a system of restorative practice which had proven fundamentally inappropriate for our setting, leaving staff very battered and bruised from the complexities of all dealing with challenging behaviour and no effective strategy to tackle it. Staff were largely onboard from the outset with the prospect of empowerment, significant SLT support and centralised systems avoiding the time consumption of behaviour. The simplicity of our systems was the key, and ensured staff could successfully apply and follow up.*

*We set aside two days of inset where we worked hard on ensuring our systems were robust and staff were informed and had had chance to practice, walk through and question the new arrangements, new systems and new software. Monday morning briefings provided staff with a particular focus or opportunity to work on based upon snags or observations from the previous week. Regular CPD after-school and Wednesday morning "Better practice briefings" retained behaviour as a key focus, reminding staff of the basics as the key thread through the first year of implementation.*

*To check and monitor the success of these new systems, initially SLT presence was significant: learning walks every lesson, visiting all lessons each period to observe the behavioural climate in the room was to the expected standard and to ensure that the system was being followed consistently across the school. Our initial feedback tended to be around the idea of not having a warning about a warning, alongside managing teachers' reluctance to send "good kids" to referral despite them not meeting behaviour expectations. The SLT presence provided reassurance to staff and ensured that any difficult situations were resolved by SLT, leaving teachers to teach.*

*To bring the pupils with us in these new routines, we delivered initial assemblies to students rolling out the "what and the why" and regularly revisited these key messages. Each term we had a reset assembly on their first day back, reminding students of the expectations and teaching them the curriculum of behaviour. The key feedback from student surveys had been that they wanted disruption free classrooms, and we promised them we would deliver this. There is no surer route to pupil buy-in than succeeding in doing what you have promised to do.*

## Robbie Russell, a Vice Principal in an all-through academy in the North of England, shares his experience of embedding routines across a school

*There is nothing worse than complicated systems in schools. Complicated systems make it harder to focus on the purpose of the task at hand due to the amount of things that need to be remembered or steps that need to be followed, even though things could be so much simpler.*

*But I don't think it needs to be like this. Reflecting on my own experiences setting up whole-school systems for routines, I think there are three steps: clarify, model and monitor. I'll try and articulate how we've done this in my context below. But before I do, I want you to learn from a mistake I made so you don't have to make it yourself. Sometimes leaders (me) are tempted to rush into the task of leadership and "improve behaviour," forgetting that behaviour is sometimes best tackled first and foremost by building student habits to ease the cognitive load of the school day so students can pay attention better and as a result learn more. Once students build strong habits through whole-school routines, they can pay attention more fully; once students are paying attention more fully, they are less likely to be "off task"; if they are less likely to be "off task," they are also less likely to behave in a way we would prefer them not to. Starting at any place in this chain of pedagogical logic other than the first step, habits formed through routines, is mistake. And one I learned the hard way. Anyway, back to the three steps.*

### Step 1: Clarify – Ask questions and develop simple answers

*The first step we took as a leadership team in developing whole-school systems and routines was to ask ourselves simple but crucial questions about "how we do things around here," ensuring that staff and students have good answers to them so that they can use them at any moment throughout the school day to encourage, correct and teach effectively.*

- *How should I behave in shared spaces? (Corridors, toilets, dining hall, outside)*

- *How should I prepare for learning?*

- *How should I learn independently?*

- *How should I learn in groups?*

- *How should I respond to feedback?*

There may be other questions that you are keen for your students to be able to answer, but the above are the ones that we focussed on as a school. These are the answers we developed.

*Q: How should I behave in shared spaces? (corridors)*

*A: Corridors: We move Silently, Safely, Sensibly (3 Ss)*

*Q: How should I learn independently?*

*A: STAR*

*Sit up straight; Track the speaker; Ask and answer questions; Respect those around you.*

*Q: How should I learn in groups? How should I talk to others?*

*A: Look; Listen; Respond*

*Look at my partner when I'm speaking; listen to them carefully; respond when it's my turn.*

   *You'll notice that I have done my utmost to ensure that the way in which we articulate how students perform whole class routines is simple, consistent and hopefully clear.*

### Step 2: Model the routine meticulously

*Modelling in Assemblies*

*Alongside a routine being shared with staff and students, it is important that it is also modelled clearly. As part of our assembly programme, I have made sure I have shown students a good and a bad example of the routine being performed, asking questions about what made each one good and bad. Sometimes I have done this with students as examples; sometimes I have done it with teachers or learning assistants. This has had a powerful impact, especially when I have coupled it with "I am coming round this week to see your STAR sitting in action and I'll let you know how we are all getting on next week." By doing this, I am able to further exemplify what our routines look like and also helps students understand I care enough about them making this happen that I will come and observe them doing this.*

*Modelling in Staff Training*

*Staff need to have the routines modelled, too. Even if they are very familiar with a routine, we all still need reminders as we work with new classes in new ways and face new challenges. It also helps as a refresher from time to time to practice a routine and ensure it is fresh in our memories.*

*Share good examples*

*Where there are good examples from moments like learning walks or observations, it is important that these are also shared with all staff so we are all clear about what excellence looks like in each and every environment.*

### Step 3: Monitor regularly

*Like I mentioned above, I try to keep my eye on routines as much as possible. When they start slipping, I know the other things probably will too. There are a few things I get leaders and staff to do and think about.*

*First, every learning walk we do includes a routines focus. We always comment on the quality of routines in each classroom whenever we give feedback to teachers. Next, I always begin each term by reminding staff about routines and if we need to practise them then we do. And finally, I always talk to students at the beginning of each term, making sure they are reminded of what to expect and how they ought to behave in shared spaced and lesson time.*

---

**In 2011, Charlie Taylor's checklist of routines was published as a simple guide for school leaders. It has since disappeared from the government website but can be found in numerous other locations**

*Key principles for headteachers to help improve school behaviour*

*Policy*

- ▪ *Ensure absolute clarity about the expected standard of pupils' behaviour.*

- ▪ *Ensure that behaviour policy is clearly understood by all staff, parents, and pupils.*

- ▪ *Display school rules clearly in classes and around the building. Staff and pupils should know what they are.*

- ▪ *Display the tariff of sanctions and rewards in each class.*

- ▪ *Have a system in place for ensuring that children never miss out on sanctions or rewards. Leadership*

- ▪ *Model the behaviour you want to see from your staff.*

### Building

- Visit the lunch hall and playground and be around at the beginning and the end of the school day.

- Ensure that other SLT members are a visible presence around the school.

- Check that pupils come in from the playground and move around the school in an orderly manner.

- Check up on behaviour outside the school.

- Check the building is clean and well maintained.

### Staff

- Know the names of all staff.

- Praise the good performance of staff.

- Take action to deal with poor teaching or staff who fail to follow the behaviour policy.

### Children

- Praise good behaviour.

- Celebrate successes.

### Teaching

- Monitor the amount of praise, rewards, and punishments given by individual staff.

- Ensure that staff praise good behaviour and work.

- Ensure that staff understand special needs of pupils.

### Individual pupils

- Have clear plans for pupils who are likely to misbehave and ensure that staff are aware of them.

- Put in place suitable support for pupils with behavioural difficulties.

### Parents

- Build positive relationships with the parents of pupils with behaviour difficulties.[4]

## The subsequent checklist for teachers from the same source might also provide helpful clarification for teachers and leaders

### *Behaviour checklist for teachers*

#### Classroom

- Know the names and roles of any adults in class.
- Meet and greet pupils when they come into the classroom.
- Display rules in the class – and ensure that the pupils and staff know what they are.
- Display the tariff of sanctions in class.
- Have a system in place to follow through with all sanctions.
- Display the tariff of rewards in class.
- Have a system in place to follow through with all rewards.
- Have a visual timetable on the wall.
- Follow the school behaviour policy.

#### Pupils

- Know the names of children.
- Have a plan for children who are likely to misbehave.
- Ensure that other adults in the class know the plan.
- Understand pupils' special needs.

#### Teaching

- Ensure that all resources are prepared in advance.
- Praise the behaviour you want to see more of.
- Praise children doing the right thing more than criticising those who are doing the wrong thing (parallel praise).
- Differentiate.

- *Stay calm.*

- *Have clear routines for transitions and for stopping the class.*

- *Teach children the class routines.*

**Parents**

- *Give feedback to parents about their child's behaviour – let them know about the good days as well as the bad ones.*

## Leading Heads of Year

Heads of Year (HoYs) are the key pastoral folk in any school. The job is relentless and can be hugely rewarding and hugely frustrating at the same time. In some schools, particularly larger ones, HoYs tend to be managed by a pastoral senior leader; however, in other schools, every senior leader will work with a year group and likely line-manage a HoY. Regardless of your leadership role, it is helpful to think through how to lead these individuals so they can have the greatest success with the young people they serve.

The HoY role is first and foremost about trust. HoYs need to build strong, trusting relationships with the pupils in their year groups, so that when any issues arise, pupils want to go to their HoY early – before they become out of control. This is the case for friendship issues and bullying; it is also the case with safeguarding concerns. HoYs need to be the ultimate firm, loving professional parent to their charges.

Given their integral role in the pastoral leadership of their year group, HoYs very often are the obvious individual to meet with families where issues have arisen, and they are often the people families reach out to for pre-emptive meetings. Bear this in mind when determining loadings for HoYs: much of their time will be spent meeting families, and this can often entail very early mornings and very late evenings to accommodate family needs. As their line manager, you will want to establish firm boundaries to support their workload and well-being: talk about their week and their working hours. The role is intensely emotional, and HoYs need strong reserves of energy to be able to cope with that – something that becomes less likely the more 14-hour days they clock up over time. HoYs, in my experience, love their year groups and will tend to agree to do anything to support their children. It is your role as their line manager to help them see that they need to first affix their own oxygen mask: saying yes to every parent meeting and every pupil request is the route to burnout.

The most helpful thing you can do when leading HoYs is to offer your time: offer to meet with tricky families. If a HoY is saying parent meetings are taking 45 minutes a time, offer to run one in 15 minutes, show how they can speed through an agenda and politely give a firm stop when the time is up: too often I've sat in meetings that are going nowhere when a shorter time frame could have prompted decisions and actions faster.

Make sure you are talking about safeguarding with HoYs. Some HoYs will be new to the role or relatively new to the profession, and safeguarding is complex and difficult to unpick. It is absolutely critical that they are making the right judgement calls when it comes to safeguarding, so ask about any issues they've been monitoring or offer some scenarios (if a child came to you and said they were locked out of their house all night, what would you say, what would you do, and whom would you tell?) to ensure they have the knowledge and awareness to do the right thing. We will go into safeguarding in more detail in Chapter 4.

Because so much of the HoY role involves firefighting, you will want to ensure that you're spending time talking to them about how they can recognise the most well-behaved pupils who are putting in impressive effort. This is important for pupils, who can feel as though the worst-behaved children get all the attention (and then, when they are in need of attention, their go-to method is obvious); it is also important for HoYs to see the full breadth of their year group and think about all the individuals, not just those who clamour to be seen and thought about.

Finally, and this may sound obvious, do meet with your HoY. I have always found that, of all the people in a school, HoYs are the hardest to pin down because they always say yes to parent meetings and they are always picking up pupils whose days aren't going well. These are the meetings they will want to skip, because to them (and rightly so) the kids are more important than their SLT line manager. Be relentless about re-booking time and try to secure time when they are unlikely to be called away – I've found earlier is better, when children are settled at the start of the day and in lessons.

---

### Sam Crome, Deputy Headteacher and Director of Education, Xavier Catholic Education Trust, shares his approach to working with Heads of Year and other pastoral leaders

*Pastoral roles in a school are fulfilling, frenetic, and demanding. They are often described as reactive, but this doesn't necessarily have to the be the case if the right systems are in place.*

*Firstly, Heads of Year must curate the culture and narrative they desire for their year group, including core values, mottos, belonging cues, reward systems, and consistent branding that is used in assembly and tutor time. The students should constantly be reminded of the year group culture, and rewarded for their contribution to this. As a leader of the Heads of Year, my role is to ensure that the culture that each Head of Year desires for their year group complements our whole-school values and ethos, so that what they promote every day aligns with the rest of the school community.*

*Their culture building potential can only be fulfilled, however, when pastoral systems ensure the consistent treatment and support of all children in the school.*

### Daily systems and protocols

*Heads of Year do a huge range of work, from being consistent with sanctions, dealing with investigations, handling safeguarding disclosures, working with parents, and responding to data, such as student attendance or behaviour points. They must make hundreds of decisions every day, and we can support their work by codifying all processes and systems. How do we respond to persistent lateness? How do we respond to incorrect uniform? What happens if someone doesn't go to detention? What happens when someone exceeds 50 house points? This consideration and follow up takes effort, but once we have crystal-clear systems, we can divide work between staff and be consistent in dealing with it. These systems should be regularly reviewed and tweaked, discussed in team meetings, and stored clearly in a handbook or in live folders on SharePoint or similar.*

### Referrals to pastoral services and interventions

*When students need extra support, there should be a centralised and clear method by which to refer them to pastoral services, such as ELSA, Home School Link Worker, Counsellors, and others. As a team, you should spend time coming up with a flowchart and process so that all Heads of Year refer students in the same manner, with regular advice to the team from pastoral services so that all Heads of Year are upskilled to understand which services would be right for their students. Ensure a clear reporting system so that the journey of the child – their needs, targets, place on waiting list, and so on – is transparent throughout, which will hopefully ensure a smooth transition after the service is complete.*

*Work with other stakeholders is critical to this process: we have so much expertise in schools, and we must consult with them to harness our shared knowledge. Heads of Year should regularly meet with the special educational needs co-ordinator (SENCO), safeguarding team, inclusion officer, and others with similar roles, to ensure that we join the dots together regarding the children's circumstances, interventions, and journey at school. We can use these discussions to improve transparency and ensure the most timely and accurate support for all children, which is then well-documented, perhaps on a secure online system like CPOMS.*

# Building on Samuel's mention of pastoral services and interventions, David Thomas shares an approach to Alternative Provision (AP) he developed while a senior leader in two multi-academy trusts

### Deciding that alternative provision is required

*Mainstream education is the right place for the vast majority of children. A small minority, however, will require more intensive support than can be offered in the mainstream classroom. For these children we should seek to meet their needs by finding appropriate placements in alternative provision. Alternative provision may be internal or external. This guide applies to use of both, although some sections are only applicable to external provision. Children attending internal provision deserve the same degree of oversight and care as those attending external provision.*

### Early engagement

*If the school believes that a child may require alternative provision then they should engage with the family and the child to discuss this before a decision is made. Schools will have processes, such as the Pastoral Support Plan, that enables this to happen. A placement in alternative provision should not come as a surprise or be a hurried decision, except in exceptional circumstances (such as a serious incident or an unexpected medical episode).*

### Considering SEND

*Nationally, over 80% of children in alternative provision have special educational needs and disabilities (SEND). The school should not consider a placement in AP without consulting the SENCo for advice on whether SEND should be further explored for that child.*

### Determining need

*A placement in alternative provision must be based on the needs of the child. It should be taken as part of a plan to ensure the child achieves their potential in education. Before agreeing to alternative provision the school must be clear on its purpose, and the end goal of any placement. For example, is this a short-term placement to support re-integration into mainstream once certain goals have been met?*

*Decisions about AP must always be taken in the child's best interests. When deciding what provision would be suitable, the school must consider:*

1 *The child's curriculum. Does it provide a solid foundation in English and Maths? If in KS3, is it broad and balanced enough to not constrain their future options? If in KS4, does it support their aspirations for post-16?*

2 *The child's social and emotional development. Does it provide opportunities to develop good habits of behaviour, such that the child will be able to re-integrate into mainstream school or to cope well in mainstream society?*

### Agreeing a provision plan

*A provision plan must be agreed by the school and the family in a meeting together. The meeting must result in a written plan with a review date no more than six weeks later.*
*During this meeting, the school should:*

1 *Agree the purpose of alternative provision, and targets that will help us know if this is being achieved*

2 *Agree the provider/s to be used, based on their ability to meet the curriculum requirements set out above*

3 *Agree that this constitutes full-time education. If it does not, they must agree arrangements for part-time, including:*

   a *What the child will be doing when they are not in education, and how they will be kept safe during this time*

   b *How the child will transition back into full-time education at the end of the specified part-time period*

4 *Agree that the curriculum studied meets the child's academic and social/ emotional needs*

5 *Record the above on an Individual Alternative Education Plan for the child, and issue a copy of this to the parent and local authority*

### Monitoring provision

*Before any external provision commences*
   *The school must:*

1 *Visit the physical location to ensure it is suitable. This includes the location being used for any individual tutoring*

2 *Review the provider's safeguarding policy, and speak to the provider's designated safeguarding lead to agree how safeguarding information will be shared between the provider and the school*

3 *Review the provider's attendance policy, and speak to the provider to agree how attendance information will be passed to the school*

4 *Review curriculum documentation showing what the child will be studying*

These checks must be recorded by the school, and signed off by a senior leader.

There should be no gap in provision between a child stopping attending mainstream classes, and starting in alternative provision.

## Attendance

It is essential that an accurate attendance record is maintained for all children, including those attending alternative provision. A named person in the school should be responsible for receiving attendance information from providers and recording this on the school's system. This information should be sent to an inbox accessible by more than one person (e.g. attendance@ schoolname.org) so that it can be accessed in case of absence. Attendance information should ordinarily be received by the school within an hour of the start of the session the child was due to attend. It must be chased if it is not received on time, so that the school can carry out safeguarding activity if they do not attend.

## Welfare checks

A child in alternative provision is the legal responsibility of the school, even if they do not attend the school site. The school must maintain a relationship with the child to support them in their duty to safeguard the child and their welfare. A child attending alternative provision must have a conversation with a member of school staff at least weekly to maintain a strong link with the school.

Children attending alternative provision are often the most vulnerable in the school. If they do not attend their provider on time then the school must contact home immediately to ascertain their whereabouts. If they do not get a response then a home visit must be conducted.

## Academic progress

The academic progress of children attending alternative provision remains the responsibility of the school. Children attending alternative provision should sit the same assessments as their peers, in the same assessment windows, for all subjects on their personalised curriculum.

## Reviewing provision

*Every child attending alternative provision should have regular review meetings at least every six school weeks. These meetings should incorporate feedback from:*

1 *The provider/s*

2 *The school*

3 *The child*

4 *The family*

*Review meetings should be focused on how the child is progressing towards the end goal set out as the reason for using alternative provision. They should take into account the views of all stakeholders on what will be needed to maximise the child's progress.*

## Children with Education, Health and Care Plans

*Schools with children who have an Education, Health and Care Plan (EHCP) who may benefit from alternative provision should familiarise themselves with paragraphs 10.39–10.46 of the SEND Code of Practice. Any alternative provision for a child with an EHCP must be commissioned by the local authority.*

*Where alternative provision is being considered for a child with an EHCP, the school must hold an annual review (or emergency annual review) in place of the meeting in the first section of this guidance. The school will need to set out why alternative provision is being considered, and why this is the best thing for the child. Where this provision would differ from the provision set out in section F of the EHCP, the school should request that the EHCP be amended. A child should not attend alternative provision unless it is clear from the current EHCP that this is the right provision for the child.*

## Annual reviews

*Of providers*
    *The school will review every provider used at least once a year. This will consist of:*

1 *Visiting the provider*

2 *Revisiting their safeguarding and attendance arrangements*

3 *Checking the progress of children who have been with that provider, and assuring themselves that the quality is high enough*

*Of use of provision*

*The school will, at least annually, review its use of alternative provision at SLT. This will include an analysis of students who have attended AP, any trends in their characteristics and the reasons they needed AP, and what progress they made towards targets.*

## Key Takeaways

◼ Take time to prepare the ground for any new initiatives.

◼ Match your routines to your context.

◼ Be mindful of the limitations and realities of your building.

◼ The stricter your routines, the more warm your team need to be in executing them.

◼ Continually raise the bar – be restless for excellence.

In the next chapter, we'll look at curriculum and the practical aspect of how leaders can manage this at a whole-school level.

## Notes

1 "Putting Evidence to Work: a school's guide to implementation" EEF, 2019. https:// d2tic4wvo1iusb.cloudfront.net/production/eef-guidance-reports/implementation/EEF_ Implementation_Guidance_Report_2019.pdf?v=1693959643.
2 Sam Strickland, *The Behaviour Manual*, p. 15 (John Catt, 2022).
3 "SLANT" is described by Doug Lemov as being an acronym for "Sit up, Listen, Ask and answer questions, Nod your head, Track the speaker"; "STAR" for "Sit up to look interested and stay engaged, Track the speaker to show other people their ideas matter, Appreciate your classmates' ideas by nodding, smiling and so on when they speak, Rephrase the words of the person who spoke before you so they know you were listening." *Teach Like a Champion 3*.0 Doug Lemov (Jossey-Bass 2021) pp. 400–402.
4 https://www.wigan.gov.uk/Docs/PDF/Resident/Education/Educational-Support/TESS/ Charlie-Taylor-checklist.pdf.

# 2 Leading curriculum

This chapter will explore all aspects of curriculum leadership, including how to support teams to create and review their curriculums and how leaders might assess whether the curriculum has been learned. We'll look at approaches to working with middle leaders on this work as well as exploring the many facets of curriculum: character curricula, literacy, early years, sixth form, special educational needs and disabilities (SEND), extra-curricular offers, and careers provision.

## Why curriculum matters

In recent years, the critical importance of the curriculum has been asserted by a wealth of educators as well as Ofsted (Office for Standards in Education, Children's Services and Skills) weighing in with their new curriculum-focused framework. Where at the start of my teaching career the "curriculum Deputy Head" tended to write the timetable and sort out rooming, it is now a much more subject-focused role, with leaders overseeing what is taught and how the plan of learning is designed. It is a tough role, particularly in secondary settings where subjects are diverse and teachers tend to be trained to teach only one of them.

Yet school leaders have responded enthusiastically to their new remit. Perhaps it is because they, too, have always sensed that curriculum is the key to a pupil's happy and successful school experience.

I was once working in a school where my remit was to improve teaching. I spent a fruitless term looking at teaching techniques, tweaking practice here and there, but not really having any impact. "Why don't we begin lessons with retrieval?" I asked one of the best Heads of Department. She looked at me quizzically. "I think I could do that. What, just what we did last lesson?" I worked with the Head of Maths after that to identify the task that pupils could do in an extended period of time. "Oh, teachers don't want them to do a lot of practice. We got rid of all the textbooks last year so it's really hard to find worksheets." She grimaced. "Probably they need more practice."

DOI: 10.4324/9781003465461-3

You can't support teachers to teach better lessons if the material they have to cover is not robust and does not lend itself to successful pupil learning. Both are important, but without a curriculum in place, it is almost impossible to teach well because, well, what are you teaching? The thing you happen to think is important? The exam specification? In one school I taught in, teachers had total autonomy to teach whatever they wanted – which was all well and good, except that every teacher ended up planning the entire curriculum from scratch, only to occasionally find, as a friend of mine did, that the class had "already done that book" with their previous teacher who had left the year before. For a whole host of reasons – both logistical and for equality of experience for pupils – a shared, central curriculum is a good idea.

With a shared subject curriculum comes a leadership responsibility to ensure that teachers are using resources and planning materials appropriately. There is a fine and sometimes fractious line to walk between allowing teachers to tailor material to best suit their particular class's needs and providing parity of experience for pupils. For example, teacher A might want to move through a unit more slowly to ensure that her weaker class grasps the material, but if they end up not covering the full unit of knowledge, they could be at a real disadvantage in future years.

In terms of what should constitute our curriculum, there are plenty of philosophical lines to be drawn: knowledge-rich or knowledge-led; pupil-led or Montessori. This book is not intending to range over this theory; however, as we go through the leadership activities, you will note that these are skewed towards consistency rather than autonomy – after all, if your philosophy is that all teachers can teach what they want, the role of the senior team in curriculum leadership is minimal.

Finally, although there are many approaches to curriculum, no single approach will work well for every subject. There is, and should be, a difference in how we plan and deliver the Maths curriculum compared with the physical education (PE) curriculum. Different subjects will have dramatically different aims and outcomes, practical and intellectual skills, larger or smaller domains of more or less complex knowledge.

## Whole-school curriculum

With the advent of Ofsted's relatively new interest in curriculum has come the omnipresence of its terms: intent, implementation, and impact. Now that schools are expected to be able to articulate these for every subject, some schools seek to prevent calamities by ensuring that these are fully documented. The articulation of a school's curriculum ordinarily is now seen in a "curriculum intent" document, which might be shared with the whole school or on its website. While colleagues will call such missives a "living document," few documents actually manage to realise this ambition, and most end up a forgotten paper exercise. Unless you intend to revisit your paper document with regularity and you find this helpful to align and inform colleagues, you would be just as well to articulate your shared aims and use these to determine any adaptations to your curriculum as the years go by. After all, the curriculum itself regularly evolves, as new knowledge enters the subject, situations change (the Geography textbook I was using in 2019 confidently claimed "the UK is part of the European Union"), or the exam spec is altered. (I will never forget my school friend going in to re-sit her English Literature AS (Advanced Subsidiary) level and finding the text she'd studied was no longer on the exam paper.)

When thinking about the whole-school curriculum, you need to ultimately consider what you want for the pupils in your school. What are the range of subjects, experiences, and extra-curricular events that will form their school experience? In doing this, you will inevitably touch on the timetable – the old favourite of curriculum leaders – to determine the balance of breadth and depth that is right for your pupils.

## The curriculum offer

School leaders are, currently, torn between playing the numbers and playing Ofsted. Playing Ofsted is more straightforward and subject to change – by this I mean having a "broad and balanced" curriculum. This is the kind of thing that Ofsted hopes prevents leaders from removing pupils from a range of subjects to ensure that they achieve better outcomes in fewer. In some schools, this looks like substituting creative subjects – Art or drama perhaps – for more Maths or English; in other schools, they offer only History or Geography, and pupils can double their time on one rather than doing both; in other schools, PE is seen as an entitlement until the lessons are commandeered in year 10 or 11 (or 9) for extra exam practice in core subjects; in other schools, pupils whose English is weak do not learn another language in Key Stage 3. It is important because we know that pupils won't get better at English by doing English 12 lessons a week, for example; they will do better in core subjects when they have a broad, strong knowledge base. E.D. Hirsch has argued at length for a rich curriculum-based approach to improving pupil attainment:

> the best way to learn lots of words is to systematically and coherently learn lots of things. The only enduring way to raise achievement and narrow gaps between groups of students is by closing the knowledge and vocabulary gap… The most egalitarian school is one that follows a cumulative, multiyear plan of knowledge building.[1]

I'm certainly not in favour of some children having a more narrow experience of the curriculum from day dot, and indeed such narrowing is counter-productive, as explained by Hirsch; however, there is a balance to be struck. My own view, and one which I'll share for transparency but acknowledge you may have valid reason to disagree with, is that there is a difference between narrowing the curriculum entitlement of an 11-year-old and a 14-year-old. With the right subject curriculum and the right teaching, I'd like to think that most 11-year-olds have a chance of success or of falling in love with a subject. Conversely, when you move into year 10 you do have a responsibility to ensure that your pupils will leave year 11 with some outcomes that they can use to further their career and personal aims. Putting a KS4 pupil through eight or nine beautifully broad General Certificates of Secondary Education (GCSEs) so they can leave with no strong passes feels somewhat unfair to me. Similarly, hoping that pupils will achieve great results through accessing only half the available subjects in the curriculum is clearly misguided: as Hirsch argues, you don't learn to read by learning reading skills – you learn by having a deep and rich knowledge of a number of domains.[2]

Curriculum leaders will need to decide how many lessons a week each subject gets, in each year group. You will want to look at your cohort and think carefully about how you can ensure that they have an opportunity to explore the wider world and build their knowledge base.

### Claire Hill, Director at Steplab and a former trust director of improvement, explores key facets of curriculum leadership here

*To ensure our curriculum makes a difference in the classroom, we need to be as focused on how the curriculum will be delivered as we are about what it includes. As a senior leader, our role is to support subject leaders to close this what-how gap, to help move from well-crafted documents detailing their intended curriculum to its effective enactment in the classroom.*

*By asking pertinent questions, a senior leader can support a subject leader to diagnose whether there are any barriers to curriculum enactment and support them to remove them. A subject leader may have a clear view of what a great curriculum looks like and have this beautifully mapped out with coherent, well-sequenced curriculum plans, that explicitly highlight key vocabulary, has clear models to demonstrate excellence for pupils and is accompanied by detailed documents and resources. But what does this excellence look like in the classroom? Is there a gap between what the subject leader hopes the curriculum will look like and the reality in practice and most importantly, how do we help them to close this gap if there is?*

*Say, for example, the subject leader has designed extensive curricular resources with lots of reading and tasks for students but has noticed these are often not completed by pupils; perhaps with pupils often 'completing' tasks by waiting for the answers from the teacher without participating or having to think hard. In assessments, students are then unable to apply what we hoped they had learnt.*

*We can see we have a problem here: our curriculum has not made a difference to what pupils know and can do. Does it mean the subject leader should change the curriculum to something students might find more interesting and therefore participate in? Do they buy presentation clickers so the teacher can circulate the room and therefore encourage participation more actively? Does the subject leader remove some of the challenge of the curriculum because perhaps it is pitched too high and that is why students aren't completing the work?*

*Problems like these are more likely to be addressed by working with the teacher on their subject knowledge so they feel confident to adapt and change the resources to ensure the focus is on learning and not just task completion, or perhaps by developing the teacher's pedagogy such as using mini-whiteboards to check understanding and prompt participation. As senior leaders, we can help subject leaders to identify the root of the problem and help create the conditions for subject leaders to address them.*

*One way senior leaders can help subject leaders to identify the real need and respond to it is to ask questions that help subject leaders to diagnose problems to solve together but also ensuring those questions help to build strong mental models for the subject leader to help them resolve similar problems in the future. Questions such as:*

- *What will it look like if pupils have learned what you intend and how can we find out if they have done so?*

- *How effectively are gaps in learning addressed through responsive teaching and/or curriculum adaptation and where might we see this in action?*

- *How well do teachers support students to think hard and participate effectively in lessons and how are they supported to do so?*

- *What models are shared and how are teachers supported to construct and deconstruct these with pupils – and what does this look like when it's effective?*

*These questions are clearly not exhaustive nor are they aimed to be asked every time leaders meet, or to be used in judgement of the subject leaders' effectiveness. Rather, they are aimed at supporting subject leaders to diagnose and solve problems by providing a space to discuss their aims and explore what this looks like in lessons, books, or conversations with teachers, teasing out whether there are gaps between the subject leaders' intentions for their curriculum and how this looks in practice. Most importantly, these conversations are aimed at developing the subject leader who in turn can develop their teachers by focusing our questions on the most important part of curriculum development: that it makes a positive difference to pupils in the classroom.*

# A word on the timetable

We'll look at timetabling more in our final chapter, because part of your whole-school curriculum consideration will encompass how these subjects are delivered. I've found it useful in previous schools to have a priority list alongside the curriculum aims. This is because timetabling is complex and you will never, sadly, achieve everything you want.

An example of a priority list might be:

Priority 1: No split classes

Priority 2: All single periods, spread across the week (i.e. no triple History on one day, so if a year 8 misses school on Tuesday, they miss their entire subject provision for the week)

Priority 3: Lowest sets in Maths have Maths lessons in the morning.

So when you come to write your timetable, above all you aren't splitting classes. Only when you've managed that do you then ensure that all lessons are single periods. Your third priority is to timetable the lowest Maths sets so they're all having Maths in the morning. Only then would you focus on other priorities.

Whatever your priorities may be, you will want to consider:

1 Number of periods in a week

2 Spread of those periods, ideally

3 Allocation across split classes – and in which year groups you might definitively *not* want split classes

4 Who teaches which stream or set if you aren't using mixed ability

# Class formation

There is a wealth of research supporting mixed-ability classes: Hattie notes "13 meta-analyses that showed students did not benefit from between-class grouping... The effects on equity outcomes are profound and negative."[3] This seems diametrically opposed to much teacher experience I've heard of, which tends to favour sets. Teachers also seem to dislike streams because they feel this is in some ways the worst of both worlds: you do not have pupils grouped by their ability in your subject, and you're allocating them by ability, leading to a "bottom" stream with all the behavioural and motivational challenges this entails.

A more optimistic framing is that streaming provides the best of both worlds: you have a group with approximately similar attitudes and aptitudes for learning, albeit with some who are stronger in other subjects and will need more support, thus making you carefully consider your instruction more than you would with a set. You have a larger group, and wider range, so even in the bottom stream you will have some children who are motivated and able to bring the rest of the group with them. Some children will struggle in different subjects, and some will find different subjects easy, making it harder for pupils to uncover what stream they are in and feel overly confident or overly unhappy about that.

## Streaming

My personal preference is for streaming, but this is probably just a corollary that the best school I worked in used streams, and none of the other schools I worked in did. I'm not a fan of sets because, no matter how you try to disguise this, pupils always find out and because the lowest sets tend, in recent years and in the schools I've worked in, to be absolutely tiny. You'd think this would be a good thing, but this quickly becomes a place where the social norms are not conducive to learning. In my experience, every "bottom" set I've taught has pupils who underachieve not because they are inherently less smart than their peers but because they do not work very hard and haven't worked hard for (probably) their entire school career. I also have found many more social and behavioural issues in these sets. This has led to children who feel negative towards school and who don't think they are capable of achieving, and I've had to work harder than is necessary with any other classes to convince them otherwise.

## The realities of pupil grouping

Mixed ability, for all its research backing, is a challenge for any teacher. I suspect the benefits are that teaching to the top (or at least the middle) means that children who might have been in a bottom set now have access to the full, rich curriculum and teaching which assumes they will grasp much of it. They will also hear great answers from their peers each lesson which help them to understand what top grades look and sound like. Behaviour norms tend to be better in a class where the most successful learners already buy into school and are happy to be there. The challenge for teachers is how to move children on and how to pitch tasks, where some will find the learning easy and be done quickly, and others will need support to access the basics. One reading of this method is that every teacher will need to adapt lesson materials, leading to higher workload for all teachers. A converse argument to this is that all classes, including sets, are mixed ability really, so teachers ought to be adapting their teaching and potentially their materials for their classes no matter how the pupils are working, and that having only a handful of pupils, say two or three, needing additional support might mean they have a chance of accessing it, compared with a class of 15 where ten require additional support.

You will need to assess the available evidence as well as your current context to determine which route to go down. I would also urge you to critically examine your current method. If you're currently mixed ability, and pupil outcomes are low and teachers are complaining about lesson planning workload, consider streams. If you are using sets and behaviour and attainment in your lowest are very poor, consider streams or mixed ability. In my experience, there is no ideal pupil grouping where teachers are happy and pupils are automatically well behaved and learning loads – but you may be able to improve on where you are.

## Creating a subject curriculum

As a senior leader, you may well have had the experience of creating a subject curriculum as a middle leader. In my first Head of English post, I bounced excitedly to my first line management meeting with my dream curriculum map in hand. My line manager's face fell. "You see, we introduced a whole new curriculum last year, so the team have had to rewrite everything for the Autumn term, and they've started on the Spring." In my second Head of English post, conversely, the entire curriculum needed to be written – which was a joy in terms of text selection and a burden in terms of resource creation.

In secondary schools, of course, middle leaders will need to consider external exams. As a senior leader, be wary of middle leaders who tell you they are covering the same material more than once because it is on the GCSE and they want pupils to do well. Because excelling in subjects involves having broad domain knowledge, repeating content rather than exploring the wider domain could have the consequence of narrowing pupils' knowledge base and ultimately stymie their achievement. At the same time, balance this with respect for your colleague: they definitely will know more than you about their subject (unless you happen to have led it as well in a previous role). I found this in leading Science: where I challenged the introduction of GCSE material in year 9, I was told by the Head of Department this was the *only* way to ensure that the full GCSE spec was covered. I sought advice from a number of other Science leaders and found that everyone seemed to be doing a version of this.

## Centralised trust curriculums

One thing you will want to make sure is that your subject leaders are able to explain the curriculum to you coherently – not for our friends at the inspectorate but because they have to know what they are teaching and why. One middle leader I worked with said: "it's the [academy trust] curriculum, so we have to teach it, even though it isn't great." What a great conversation starter! I'm not sure you can confidently lead a team of teachers in ensuring that the curriculum is planned to move pupils on if you ultimately think your curriculum is "not great." We worked hard to clarify what about the centralised curriculum wasn't working and to understand the adaptations and additions we could implement to make it better. (It turned out, lots – some multi-academy trusts [MATs] seem to have a set-in-stone curriculum which, on further investigation, is actually being adapted by many schools to ensure it's as good as it can be.)

So, if your middle leaders are working with a centralised curriculum, your role is to help them understand how to "own" this, supporting them to adapt it in any way required to assure them it is providing the best subject experience for the particular pupils in your setting, and brokering meetings between them and the central team if concerns are more pressing on their part. If you are not a subject expert in their area, it can be hard to determine which of their concerns are genuine and which are preference, but with some digging, reaching out to any trusted past colleagues in this subject, and an open, honest conversation with the Trust subject lead, you should get to a better place.

## Rewriting the curriculum

There will be other instances where you will line-manage departments who are writing or rewriting a curriculum. In the very rare circumstance of starting a school from scratch, a large part of your leadership role is to oversee the creation of a curriculum. In more usual circumstances, colleagues will be writing a curriculum to replace what they have. This will happen when the GCSE specification changes or updates, when their curriculum is identified by external individuals as being in need of improvement, when you are moving from a highly autonomous school where teachers can choose to teach what they like to a more streamlined process of a shared curriculum, or when a new Head of Department is appointed and they see how the curriculum can be changed to better serve the pupils in your school.

Although a large part of this process will be around leading their team (which we will explore later in this chapter), you will also need to sense-check their work. Use open questions and be genuinely curious about their subject. Ask why this unit, why in this order, how does it build on the previous unit? Ask what the core knowledge is for each unit and how they will revisit that knowledge in later units to secure it for the long term?

The other process aspects of this work will be ensuring that colleagues have the time and space required to do this work. Help them to allocate out parts of the work to individuals who are well placed to do it, and ensure they are particularly avoiding overburdening Early Career Teachers. Unless you have exceptional circumstances, I would probably advocate leaving trainee teachers alone for this work – the work of crafting a curriculum is complex, and it is a rare trainee who is able and ready to take part in it.

Make sure you have checked the curriculum sequence and unit sequence prior to commencing writing. It is a huge piece of work, and the last thing you want to do is to tell colleagues part way that you think they're going down the wrong path with something.

## Reviewing a subject curriculum

If your school is not creating a new curriculum, part of your role in managing subject leads is to regularly review the existing curriculum, which will require minor or major updates or rewrites from time to time. This relies on a strong, trusting relationship with your subject lead, particularly if they themselves have had a part in writing the initial curriculum. It is incredibly tough to critique our own work.

Ideally, this review forms part of a whole-school process, so your middle leader doesn't feel targeted in any way, and you aren't seen as over-zealous. If a process doesn't exist, push your leadership team to adopt one. It can, and should, be simple, and at a time of year that makes sense – probably not in the run-up to national exams, for instance.

In working to review the curriculum, leaders should be supporting teams to think about what is taught, when, and how. You will need to first establish the key big ideas within the subject, so you can sense-check whether this curriculum meets the goal of delivering on these. For example, you might look at the sequence of units taught in History across seven years in a secondary school. Think through the sequence: is it supporting pupils to make connections between periods? Is it supporting pupils to develop a sense of chronology? Are they being introduced to sources in a way that makes sense given their knowledge and ability to interpret them as well as given the work they will need to be able to do with them at national assessments?

Are there too many units? Having too much crammed into a curriculum makes it less likely that pupils will be able to truly grapple with ideas and learn key knowledge for the long term. A History curriculum which covers World War II in just three weeks of two lessons a week is likely to result in shallow learning. Too few? Having too thin a curriculum could lead to pupils not developing a robust schema of core knowledge. An English curriculum where pupils read just three texts in an entire academic year might not allow them to read broadly enough to develop their schema. At the same time, both of these hypothetical approaches might be exactly right for your particular school context.

## Core knowledge

Within units, what core knowledge is learned by pupils and tested in later units, terms, and years? Sense-check whether this is reasonable, given the breadth of knowledge that pupils will need to acquire over all the many subjects they are learning. You can also sense-check how this is going to be learned: assuming that children will learn core knowledge as homework and revise it unprompted and without teacher quizzing to hold them to account is unlikely to lead to lasting memory retention.

With core concepts, how are these developed and revisited in ever more complex ways? Is the content challenging enough for your most able pupils? Is there enough scaffolding to enable all pupils to access it?

It is always sensible to check the exam specification for the subject and to ensure that your curriculum is preparing pupils for success at both GCSE and A level. Some schools will also check the year 1 university course to ensure that children are being prepped for eventual success effectively. Exam specifications change over the years, and where leaders can make unit choices what was right once may not still be, particularly given teacher turnover and any pupil context changes, so be ready to have a robust conversation about why leaders have chosen the option units they have.

Ensure that reviewing a curriculum is not reviewing a document and that you aren't adding to middle leader workload by requiring all of the above to be presented in document form. It would be better to simply allocate a chunk of time to talk about these ideas with your middle leader one to one, and dig into a very large sample of lessons to see if the stuff pupils are doing matches the things they are talking about. Even better would be to have access to pupil books across the ability and age range, so you can see whether pupils are or are not having success with the curriculum as it stands.

---

### Matt Burnage, Assistant Principal at Ark Soane Academy, shares an approach to supporting continual curriculum improvement

*One of the challenges of leading a school is that so much of what we do is amorphous and difficult to measure. In some cases, this is because the number of components contributing to a given educational outcome is vast, making it difficult to disentangle and identify the particular impact of any given component. In other cases, the problem is that the thing we want to measure is largely invisible to us.*

*The curriculum – the sequence of knowledge that our students encounter over the course of their time at school – is amongst the trickiest areas to unravel. However, it is of central importance that we are able to unpick and analyse it. With the exception of keeping our students safe, the curriculum is the single most important thing that we offer our students, and is the sole area in which schools have a unique role that is not taken up by any other individual or organisation in society. As a result, we have a duty to work to ensure that the content of our curriculum is ambitious, well suited to our pupils, well sequenced, and is landing well in classrooms.*

*Because of the inescapable difficulty of making any objective judgement about the quality of our curriculum, the best thing we can do in our leadership of the curriculum is worth to ensure that the curriculum is improving. If we are confident that each department is making meaningful bets that are seeking to improve and refine their curriculum, then we can at least be confident that we're moving in the right direction. We therefore need to seek to build a quality assurance model around a process of working alongside our Heads of Department to ensure that we are identifying potential areas of weakness, and making sensible decisions about how to address them.*

### Identifying where to improve

The first step in improving the curriculum is to identify areas that are sub-optimal. Heads of Department will already have long lists of things that they would like to change or improve about their curricula, but as we do not have unlimited time, we need be assiduous about how we use that which we do have.

In your first weekly meeting with a Head of Department that you line-manage, you might start by asking them what areas of the curriculum they want to prioritise this half-term. Bear in mind the experience of the person you are working with – a strong Head of Department may already have a clear idea about what their priorities should be. If your Head of English tells you that he is worried about how well students are grasping Shakespeare, you might ask:

1   What is giving you the impression that students are struggling? What have you seen in their assessments/exercise books/answers in class?

2   Is this a weakness for the whole cohort? Or are some classes struggling more?

3   What do you think is causing this weakness? Why?

### Supporting newer leaders

If we are working with a middle leader who is newer to role, we may need to offer more support through our questioning to help them identify their priorities in the first instance:

1   Let's talk about the Year 8 curriculum – what do you think is landing well? What isn't?

2   Was there anything in their last assessment results that concerned you? Were there any particular areas of weakness?

3   Are there any particular groups of students whose performance is a concern? Why?

   a   Year groups

   b   Low/medium/high attainers

   c   Students with special educational needs

   d   English as an Additional Language (EAL) students

### Involve the team

In both instances, we might ask our Heads of Department to take the discussion back to their teams – they are likely to want the collective knowledge *of their entire team to support this discussion. This is a good thing and we should not shy away from it – the more minds we have working to identify the problem, the closer we are likely to get to a good solution.*

### A spirit of inquiry

*Once we have supported our newer Head of Department in identifying an area they can focus on, we can begin to support them in working through a similar set of questions to our experienced Head of Department. At this point, our work must become investigative. We need to spend time working with our Head of Department and their team to look into not only what the precise problem is, but also to be confident that the problem that they have identified really is a problem. The way we go about investigating this problem will vary depending upon the area under discussion, but there are a number of types of evidence that we might want to consider as part of our investigating:*

| Evidence | Questions we might ask |
|---|---|
| Exercise books | What can you see in students' work that might give you an insight into how well they are learning x? What common errors can you see across a class/cohort? |
| Student assessments | What things do students seem to be commonly getting wrong? If sitting a common assessment as part of a multi-academy trusts (MAT) or group of schools – how have our students performed relative to those in other schools? What are our relative strengths/weaknesses? |
| Student responses in lessons | What are teachers seeing when teaching topic x? What things are students seeming to struggle with in lessons? |
| Student panels | What are students saying about what they find difficult? Take time to ask students extra questions about the area we are investigating to unpick the problem. Note: use student voice with caution – we must be wary of the validity of student self-reporting. |

*This challenge to investigate is vital, and it is this that can enable us to bridge the gap between our specialist Head of Department and our (potentially non-specialist) position as a senior leader. Our goal is to challenge the claims – not out of an assumption of inaccuracy or ineptitude, but to ensure that the things that we ask our Heads of Department to work on are high-leverage and worth their limited time. If, throughout our investigations we repeatedly ask ourselves the question "how do we know?", not only can we be confident that we are addressing a real problem, we also force our discussion to stay close to the substance of the curriculum (i.e. what students are learning).*

*We must keep investigating until we are confident of two things. First, that the problem we are spending time on is a concern – and is a relatively important one. Second, that we have enough detail about the problem to be able to identify actions that we can take that we are confident will lead to improvement of the curriculum. If our investigations lead us to believe that the problem we were initially grappling with is actually relatively minor, then we might begin to investigate another area through the same process.*

### Identify actions

*Once we are confident that we have identified an area that we want to spend time improving, we need to identify the concrete actions that we want to take to improve the curriculum. Because we are now confident that we are grappling with a significant concern, these actions can serve as a department's strategic priorities for a coming term or half-term.*

*As with setting any actions, we must ensure that these actions are specific and time-bounded. What these actions look like is, of course, likely to significant vary depending on the nature of the problem, but they may include the following:*

- *Re-teaching a key idea or topic in the immediate term*

- *Re-planning part of the curriculum to address an area of weakness in the medium/long-term, so that the area is revisited in the future*

- *Re-planning the curriculum for the next cohort to pre-empt the problem (this could be replanning the section where an idea was taught suboptimally, or including further opportunities to encounter it earlier or later in the curriculum)*

- *Training within the department team to ensure that all members of the team are confident in teaching the topic*

### Next steps

*In identifying these actions, there are a few important challenges that we must face. One of these is the fact that any plans we put in place to improve the curriculum are, inevitably, bets. It is not possible to be certain that any changes we make to the curriculum will be better than what was there previously. Our investigative focus can help us here by helping us to be more confident that we have identified a genuine area of weakness, but we must embrace a degree of uncertainty about any solution. In agreeing out our next steps, we must therefore opt for those things that seem most likely to improve things.*

*The second challenge is one for us as senior leaders. It is likely that these actions are likely to feel relatively small-scale when compared to the vast complexity of a five or seven-year curriculum. Our instinctive view of the school from a long-term perspective may tempt us to feel that we are tinkering at the edges of much bigger problems. In rare cases this may be true, but if we attempt to focus on too big a problem, we risk losing a meaningful focus on the substance. The closer we are to a problem, the better our solution is likely to be. We must therefore accept that our attempts to improve the curriculum are likely to consist of a series of rigorously planned small steps rather than grand initiatives.*

*At the end of a term (or whatever time period we select for this process), Senior Leadership Team (SLT) can come together and discuss the priorities identified by each department. This serves several purposes. First and foremost, it keeps SLT informed about the strengths/weaknesses and priorities of each department, which can inform their thinking about school improvement. Second, it may shed light on some whole-school priorities. Have multiple departments identified a weakness with Year 8? Are English, History and Geography all struggling with the weakest readers in Year 7? Where such commonalities exist, we may be able to support departments through whole-school solutions (equally, we may not).*

## Assessment: in class, informal, formative

In this chapter, we will first explore in-class, informal assessment before moving onto more formal, in-school assessment points. We will take formal, external examinations as a given and instead look at how these can be managed operationally in our final chapter.

We will begin with formative assessment, which should be the backbone of your school's curriculum and teaching.

It is easy for leaders to become obsessed with summative assessment. This is particularly true the higher up in leadership you go, because the less you are on the ground in schools, the more you seek some kind of unknowable objective truth about what is happening in them. We will cover the challenges of securing reliable data below, but here we will just reiterate that the most important aspect of assessment is teachers finding out what pupils don't know or can't do yet and doing something about it.

In your interactions with teachers, make sure you are more interested in this than any numbers on a page. Your teachers need to get the message *not* that they should be prepping their classes for occasional tests and fixating on these but that their day-to-day work of asking questions and adapting their teaching when they hear the answers is where you want them to be putting their time, effort, and focus.

# What to look for

Your work as a leader need be no more than having a look at books together and walking around lessons. You're definitely not looking for marking – I've written extensively in *Simplicity Rules* that this is a burdensome practice with only marginal gains. What you are looking for is two-fold: one, that the pupils' work seems to be getting better, which means either the quality of what they are writing improves over time or you can see the work they are being set and being successful at is getting more difficult over time. The former is likely in subjects like English or History, where pupils are likely to do similar tasks the whole school year, but they will, we hope, be writing higher-quality answers as the year goes on, because they've had great feedback on how to make their work incrementally better.

The other thing I look for in books is whether teachers are asking recap questions, so I can see that they are revisiting the curriculum. Where you say that teachers do this orally, I would be concerned that not 100% of pupils are answering every question – and if you start your lesson with recap, as many professionals now do, pupils who are late may miss this critical aspect of learning. I've always insisted that recap answers be written as single words where possible so the recap is brief and swift and self-marked by pupils. Personally, I do these at the back of exercise books so this work is distinct from their extended pieces and also to save space, because wasting five lines for five one-word answers feels like not the kind of thing you should be doing when the planet is on fire, but in the back of their books, you can rule the page into columns and get three or four times as many answers on those same five lines over time.

Don't confine your work on formative assessment to books. Pupils' written work will not reveal everything about the way their teachers are responding to their current needs and gaps. Try to visit classrooms regularly together and have one visit focus on formative assessment, where you listen out for the quality of teacher questioning and have a follow-up on how they might adapt their future planning to cater for any needs or gaps that surfaced.

# Assessment: in school, formal, summative

As senior leaders, you have a responsibility to ensure that any assessment you ask teachers to do is more worthwhile than the teaching that they would have done in that time. Pupils using a lesson to sit an assessment, and any lessons or homework spent preparing for it, has to matter, because time is precious and children can't afford to waste a lesson taking a nonsense assessment that doesn't move their learning on and doesn't give you robust data on which to base decisions.

The most important aspect of assessment, including summative assessment, is that pupils receive feedback about it that moves their learning on. With any assessment where they are given a grade, however, the evidence suggests they are unlikely to take on board feedback to improve.[4] One colleague of mine would mark his pupils' exams without putting any scores or numbers on the paper, instead logging them on his own spreadsheet, and go through the entire paper with them, sharing their grades after this was done. Whatever you choose for your context, if you can find a way to withhold grades or scores until after feedback, you would help pupils to get more learning out of the experience.

## Designing assessments

In terms of designing assessments, it is extremely challenging for lone schools, and lone teachers, to do this well enough to generate data that is valid and reliable. Any assessment you give that is validated (for example, a GCSE paper with mark scheme and grade boundaries) will be preferable – though, even then, teachers marking their own papers are unlikely to be able to preclude the human biases that plague us all. A standardised assessment bought in from a company will give you more valid and reliable data, by virtue of both the mark scheme having no room for ambiguity (right/wrong answers) and the number of pupils across the country who are sitting it; a drawback is that such assessments will rarely align with your in-school curriculum.

There will be senior leaders who tend to one of two extremes on assessment: either they meticulously craft assessments in house and convince themselves the data is rich and valid, and proceed to analyse it as if it were actual summative standardised data, or, on the other extreme, they buy in an assessment and proceed to act as if that is the verdict on their own curriculum.

Ultimately, neither method will give you what you actually need to know: is your curriculum moving pupils on so they will be successful in their nationally standardised exams? Is your curriculum robust enough that it sets pupils up for success in later life?

Unfortunately, only time will tell if pupils are on the right track for this. My personal view is that I think pupils sitting some form of formal test in test conditions is important for other reasons: it prompts them to work hard revising what they have learned, which puts them in a good position for all their future exams of importance. It allows them to feel comfortable in exam conditions by the time exams that really matter roll around. And it should lead to them learning something about how they can continue to improve.

My advice to senior leaders tends to be to get teachers to focus on these aspects of assessment: habit forming, revision and hard work, and filling knowledge gaps post-assessment. Any work analysing such data sets or rebuilding a curriculum in response to a bought-in test is likely to be misguided.

## Tom Clements, Assistant Headteacher at Roundhay School, explains how his school has adapted their Key Stage 3 Assessment model

*Like many leadership teams, we weren't entirely satisfied with the Key Stage 3 assessment system that we had adopted following the abolition of National Curriculum Levels in 2014. While it provided a measure of progress across subjects, it didn't tell us what we needed to know to drive progress at this crucial stage of our pupils' education.*

*We decided to address this in early 2020 and returned to it throughout the disruption caused by the pandemic. Our principles were that any changes had to provide clarity about progress to pupils and parents, that we would ensure consistency between subjects and we would avoid any unnecessary increase in teacher workload.*

*We established that our assessment system had to allow us to identify pupils who were not yet ready for Key Stage 4 study and also, more crucially, identify the specific barriers that were preventing this progress. Together, we came up with the following system:*

| Key Barrier | How we measured this |
| --- | --- |
| *Are pupils numerate?* | ■ *Key Stage 2 Standard Assessment Tests (SATs) results*<br>■ *Nationally benchmarked assessments at the start of Year 7 and the end of Year 9*<br>■ *Maths internal teacher assessment* |
| *Are pupils literate (including reading fluency)?* | ■ *Key Stage 2 SATs results*<br>■ *Nationally benchmarked assessments at the start of Year 7 and the end of Year 9*<br>■ *English internal teacher assessment* |
| *Are pupils ready to learn?* | ■ *Average teacher assessed effort grades awarded in each subject*<br>■ *Separate score for effort inside and outside the classroom* |
| *Are pupils able to recall core knowledge?* | ■ *Knowledge recall tests to take place in key subjects twice per year*<br>■ *Only take place in subjects where there is a high proportion of knowledge* |
| *Are pupils on track to be ready for KS4 study?* | ■ *Internal teacher assessment in each subject based on 'age-related expectations'*<br>■ *Averages collected for core, English Baccalaureate (EBacc) and 'Open Bucket' subjects* |

*Now that we had a system in place, the essential next step was to put in place an effective process that would allow us to achieve our core purpose of removing barriers to learning so that our pupils would be able to make excellent progress during Key Stage 3. This led to the creation of two additional meetings: Key Stage 3 Forum and Year Team Around the Child (YTAC).*

*YTAC is a group of staff that meets after each data collection to look in granular detail at each pupil in the school. The staff who gather are the people who know the children best including the Head of Year, a Pupil Premium Lead, the special educational needs and/or disabilities coordinator (SENDCO) and coordinators in English and Maths. We identify pupils who the data tell us are most in need of support and intervention to overcome one of the barriers outlined above. They are then prioritised by need and interventions are put in place before we review success at the next mid-year report.*

*The Key Stage 3 Forum, on the other hand, is the engine room of Key Stage 3. We gather all staff from departments with a specific Key Stage 3 responsibility which for us means English, Maths, Science, Languages, History, Geography and Inclusion. We look at patterns in the data and use our collective wisdom to develop strategies for use in the classroom to address these concerns. Staff then take these ideas back to their department meetings to train colleagues so that we can collectively raise standards across our subjects. This is then followed up through calendared quality assurance.*

*This has allowed us to ensure that Key Stage 3 has become more responsive to pupil need. We have been able to address specific problems quickly – addressing individual barriers through intervention – and collectively – implementing key strategies across the curriculum.*

---

**Becky Jones, Assistant Headteacher (Achievement) at Churchdown School Academy in Gloucestershire, shares how her school managed a change to fewer formal assessment points in an academic year**

*As a large non-selective secondary school catering for over 1400 pupils, we need to collect accurate and precise data to support our pupils in achieving the very best outcomes. Accurate and precise data is essential to inform the next steps in both teaching in the classroom as well as offering targeted interventions. Our focus on assessment came about from the need to have conversations about students' achievement, but also knowing that all teachers needed to know with pinpoint accuracy what students could do well, and what they needed more support with. As a result, we decided to implement an assessment calendar that mapped out three key points across the year where assessments would take place for each year group, including our sixth form.*

*We have internal year group exams once a year that are already on the school calendar and take place in our school hall and gym that are fixed, but beyond this, whilst I sent out a suggested template to Heads of Department, they had the autonomy to place assessments where they thought fitted best in terms of their curriculum plans. Moving to three key assessment points reduced the pressure on teachers and Heads of Department to continually assess in a summative way and thus reduced the formal marking load quite significantly. This was well received by all staff which helped to achieve greater buy-in when we were asking for the assessment processes to become much more forensic in both their design and follow up.*

*Understandably, if we assessed what students knew at only three points across the year, it would not be responsive and so teachers also regularly start their lessons with retrieval and multiple-choice questions, and then use their time in the classroom live marking and responding to misconceptions as they occur instead of taking away teaching time by constantly assessing in a formalised way.*

*In order to ensure that the more formal assessments were eliciting the information needed, myself and another colleague devised a Standard Operating System (SOS) for assessments and exams. Within this, we included simple steps that all Heads of Department had to follow to ensure that the assessments were all suitable – for example, specifying that mid-year exams at Key Stage 4 needed to follow a similar structure to the terminal exams they would face. We also ask that the assessments are delivered blind, so that only the Head of Department knows what the questions will be, as we realised that prior to this some unconscious (or maybe conscious!) bias was creeping into lessons before assessments which then skewed the data. We ask for copies of the exams to be forwarded to the line manager on a set date (dates are sent out at the start of the year so that middle leaders can effectively plan for these) and these are brought to our leadership team meeting where we check content and format asking the questions: what data will this assessment provide us with? How will we use this?*

*We acknowledged that assessment design was only part of the picture however, and how these papers were being marked was just as, if not more, important. To this end, we delivered training to all staff about standardisation and moderation processes. We have dedicated continuing professional development (CPD) time as a school on a Monday evening every week and on assessment weeks, we ensure that teams have two hours dedicated to standardisation and require that all teachers responsible for marking assessments attend this prior to marking the mid-year exams. We also ask, as per our SOS for exams, that Heads of Department pull a sample of marking early on in the assessment window to just check that the agreed standard is being consistently applied. Data is then centrally uploaded to departmental trackers and copied into the school's management information system (MIS) and post-moderation, if the marking of assessments needs to be amended, then this happens prior to any analysis taking place.*

*In order to complete the assessment cycle, at least one lesson is required to be devoted to feedback which also demands that students complete some follow up work to action this feedback and allows teachers to strengthen further their knowledge of the class's strengths and weaknesses. This therefore means that when students complete another piece of work the teacher can give some whole class feedback and check whether progress against the areas of weakness has been made.*

*The other two assessment points are slightly different to the mid-year exams in that they are not so formalised. As a leadership team, we recognised that sometimes students were only being assessed on their most recent learning and therefore some of the knowledge was not being committed to long-term memory. In order to combat this, we asked that at KS3 that the assessments follow a three-section structure:*

- *Section A: Knowledge testing (this section could also be marked in class to reduce marking load),*

- *Section B: Application of skills and knowledge from the most recent learning, and*

- *Section C: Synoptic assessment of knowledge and skills learnt earlier in the year and key stage.*

*This not only supported Heads of Department with assessment design, but also meant that the students were aware of the format of assessments across the curriculum.*

*This may feel like quite a lengthy process, yet it only happens formally three times a year. Last year, our headteacher also made the decision to increase the number of inset days that we have as a school. At leadership team level, we discuss, as a group, where we should place these inset days and try, wherever possible, to place one following KS4 and KS5 assessments. This gives teachers dedicated standardisation and marking time. These days allow teachers the time to mark and discuss papers with one another and avoids teachers having to rush through their marking load.*

## Chris White, a Head of Maths in Oxfordshire, explores how assessment was embedded in a regular homework routine in his school's Maths department

*When I joined the school in September 2021, I inherited a Maths department with a well-established feedback system for formative assessments which forensically tracked student performance and then guided them to follow up on Sparx, the Maths homework platform. I was unhappy with this because, in practice, the follow-up was not effective. Feedback was stored in books which remained in the classroom, and there was no imperative to complete the work – no push from the students' motivation nor pull from the ethos of the school. We improved our communication of the rationale, and the imperative from the teachers in class, but I felt that it remained ineffective, and that student independence and motivation was not improving.*

*A separate challenge was that heavy use of mini-whiteboards meant that books seen in isolation would not demonstrate a curriculum journey. I was concerned about a deficit of written maths and note-taking, which aligned with student complaints that they needed more support with homework.*

*Mindful of the unexpected consequences of change in a complex school environment, I knew it would be important to spend time watching and waiting, discovering where a new idea (or problem) "fits." Holding these ideas and problems together like pebbles in your mind over time can really help to shape them, so that the solution hits that sweet spot where it has multiple positive effects on the system. And so, my personal pebbles included student motivation, written maths, independence, and acting on feedback.*

*In a department meeting, I proposed the idea of a "home book" to be used for worked examples and taken home by students. As well as improving written notes and supporting homework, this book would also store the follow-up from assessments. We also agreed a change to our assessment regime whereby students complete and review a pre-test in class, before spending a week's homework revising, and then doing the "real" test. They would then receive follow-up feedback that they could keep.*

*We hoped that by using a large chunk of curriculum time and placing learning goals front and centre, students would be less concerned with performance. Giving them the test in advance would demonstrate that it was a truly developmental process and have a marked effect on their motivation. A secondary, but important, effect was that it allowed us time to coach independence; to teach them how to revise and for them to practise it.*

*Staff buy-in was built through collaboration, remaining mindful of process fairness. The idea aligned with the established values of the department and was developed in an open forum, which led to a strong commitment from teachers and therefore, vitally, a consistent and well-informed delivery to students.*

*Curriculum timings were adjusted to allow sufficient space. This took a significant amount of consideration and ultimately, we needed to accept the hypothesis that some later topics would take less time due to improved prior knowledge. Making the assessments themselves was already "in the budget" of time. Two tests take longer than one but in practice this was easier than expected and certainly not double the time cost.*

> *It is early days, but after cycle 1, teachers are reporting better commitment from students at all attainment levels, a frustration-driven determination to improve specific topics, and better motivation to work hard to do well. Students see the point, feel strongly about their ability to improve and – bonus – they have two chances to prove it to themselves. The odds are stacked in their favour with no loss of formative data.*
>
> *We are not complacent though and ideas for further improvement abound. Why not have the pre-test as open-book? This would stress-test their note-taking. Why not have the two tests a week apart? This would ensure revision equity.*
>
> *The hope is that by holding self-improvement at the heart of our curriculum and community, and prioritising learning over performance, we will improve confidence in the power of effort and finally change some belief systems.*

## Leading subject leaders

For most senior leaders, a key part of the role is to lead subject leaders. If you have done the Head of Department role yourself, there are some benefits and challenges to that. Leading a new subject head in a job you have done can feel supportive, as you can anticipate the challenges and scaffold their thinking. However, many middle leaders feel caught between two places: trying to please SLT and trying to please their department. In some cases, SLT support can be experienced as a lack of autonomy. Take time to check in on their thinking.

I've written in *Culture Rules* about Kim Scott's *Radical Candour*, which I'd advise any leader to read. Building strong relationships with your subject leaders is critical, especially because they are the people who can tell you with incredible accuracy how whole-school policies are playing out "on the ground." There will be many Heads of Department watching new initiatives crash and burn and thinking "if anyone had asked me, I would have told them why this was a terrible idea." So ask them. Genuinely ask them. Don't just seek permission for something you were going to do anyway. Welcome feedback and model taking it on.

With middle leaders who are uncomfortable giving feedback to their line manager, you will need to practice and ask for feedback more times than feels sensible. I've taken to parroting "feedback is a gift" and giving *myself* feedback in front of them to start them off: "I was thinking I probably could have set this task up in a better way, because it feels like the timescales are a little challenging for some people – how have you found them?" Say the mistake you suspect you made and you can often unlock all the other stuff you didn't realise you did wrong.

## Balance administration with the core business

Being a Head of Department (HoD) can often feel like quite a process-driven checklist job. There is a huge amount of administration associated with the role, particularly where multiple exam qualifications are being run by the subject team. As SLT, try to add as little as is necessary to the role in terms of administration. It is better to put in more time than more documents. For example, if you want your HoD to conduct a load of learning walks to check quality and consistency of teaching, it would be better to schedule time to do these, ensuring that your HoD is covered so they can see all teachers teaching, and then set aside a whole line management meeting to debrief on these. Even better, do them together. In a couple of schools I led in, we had to spend the first 15 minutes of line management walking the subject corridor. Make it a habit and it won't overtake the meeting, because you'll be touching base on something you see together all the time.

## Using time wisely

One aspect you will most likely need to check in with your HoD is around workload. HoDs tend to be fiercely protective of their teaching teams, which can translate to them doing the work that should more reasonably be spread across the team. It is reasonable to ask teachers to undertake some planning for the department, particularly if those teachers are going to benefit from a shared, centralised curriculum.

In many schools, HoDs will have a team meeting to run, more or less regularly. Work on co-planning how this time will be spent and be especially alert for anything making the agenda that could be an email with follow-up. The ideal use of this time is for HoDs to train their teachers to deliver better lessons or to look at pupil work and understand the best practice of colleagues that has supported young people to produce this. Help HoDs to prioritise this, and never be the person who fills their agenda with meaningless administrative chores.

A key concern in increasing numbers of departments is teachers who have a foot in two roles. HoDs will continue to be frustrated by Heads of Year and SLT who happen to teach their subject but rarely (in my experience) prioritise attending department meetings. Ensure SLT model that attendance is non-negotiable, and follow up with their people if they are not attending. Where teachers teach, say, mainly Maths and a couple of lessons of Economics a week, help HoDs to schedule meetings that ensure they can attend both or catch up on one – and genuinely be able to do that. (If we're asking people to attend two hours of meetings and not one, something does have to give to free up that time.)

In many departments, particularly with the challenges of teacher recruitment at the present time, HoDs will have teachers who are not subject experts. These teachers will need additional subject knowledge support, so work with your HoD to identify the reading and other preparatory work that they can do, and that is reasonable for them to do, to be ready to deliver a great curriculum experience to young people.

## The non-academic curriculum

All schools have a statutory and moral responsibility to teach young people the skills and knowledge necessary to exist in the modern world. This curriculum tends to be called something like PSHE (Personal, Social, Health, and Economic education). In some schools I've worked at, this extends itself to the soft skills and study skills needed to succeed in future employment – and we'll talk more about careers education later on in this chapter.

Much as schools are overburdened with the general public determining that they should be the conduit for teaching everything from sewing to cooking to public speaking and the ins and outs of mortgages, it is a truth generally accepted that in some schools if pupils do not learn this critical information in the school, they may not learn it at all.

I would strongly advise schools to have someone lead this curriculum in a HoD role. After all, it is the sole curriculum that every child in the school without exception will experience and that the widest variety and number of teachers are likely to teach. It can be, and is in some schools, a complete waste of pupils' time. By outlining the curriculum aims and delineating its sequence, you stand a better chance of giving pupils something meaningful and useful in the time allocated.

Asking pupils what they want on such a curriculum, or any curriculum, is not something I would advocate. That said, sixth formers are a particular exception: year 13 stand on the brink of the real world, a scary and unknown place, and are beginning to understand where their knowledge gaps might be. It is worth speaking to sixth formers about what they feel they need to be able to know and do to confidently go into the wider world. I once consulted sixth formers who said they were frustrated that PSHE was "all about national and international issues" – a particular slant in the school I worked in where we wanted to expand pupil horizons – but that they had no idea how to cook a meal or look for somewhere to rent and budget for being able to afford it.

With all curriculums, leaders will bring their own biases to bear on their text and idea selection. With PSHE, it is especially important that this be tempered with many adult minds to sense-check that the taught material is genuinely of importance and use for the young people in the building. Take a critical view of the curriculum and seek other opinions, but don't be swayed by someone's personal experience or lack of being translated into overcompensation in this way.

# Rob Orme, Vice Principal at Ark Soane Academy, writes about their approach to the non-academic curriculum

*Authentic character development supports students to be successful in their lives and can transform the culture of a school, but shaping the character of hundreds or more students each day is no small task. It requires more than simply mapping out which assemblies, tutor times and PSHE lessons will cover particular traits or virtues. It needs to permeate every aspect of school life. Character is not just learned about, but lived in routines, rituals and interactions between students and staff. The steps we have taken to develop character at Ark Soane are below.*

1 ***Clarity:*** *To determine what character traits to promote, we looked to our school mission and values. In no particular order, we decided on "hard working, kind, aspirational, confident, considerate, good-mannered, generous, articulate, organised, inquisitive, grateful and resilient, all underpinned by a sense of personal responsibility." Others would choose differently. The important thing is to have a clear, shared vision about what kind of character the school wishes to encourage, for if this isn't driven by adults, the vacuum will inevitably be filled by the most influential students.*

2 ***Staff Training:*** *Staff buy-in to the importance of developing the character traits is essential, but staff also need to know how they can practically mould and reinforce good character in the interactions they have with students each day. There is no point teaching students to be considerate in PSHE but allowing them to leave mess on their tables at lunch. There is no point teaching students to be polite in assembly if adults allow them to walk past without greeting them, or speak to them without using please and thank you. Therefore, staff are given concrete examples of things to be vigilant for including phrases, body language, facial expressions, and ways of addressing and responding to them. Staff practice scenarios and are taught how to correct impoliteness in a way that de-escalates, typically by conveying that they assume the child has made a mistake rather than behaved defiantly.*

3 ***Explicit Teaching:*** *At the start of Year 7, students have a four-day induction to explicitly teach them the why the Ark Soane characteristics matter. They also learn how they can demonstrate these traits through their school day in order to build strong character-forming habits. The key messages from induction are reinforced through two 30-minute tutor times across their first half term at the school. All year groups have an "induction reboot" lesson with their tutor at least once every term which is normally at the start of a half term.*

4 ***Routines:*** *Most students will not become more kind, grateful or organised people simply because of a one-off lesson or assembly each half term. They need to be in an environment that provides repeated opportunities to enact these things and to receive praise for doing so. As Aristotle wrote, "we are what we repeatedly do." Therefore, we manufacture opportunities through routines that enable students to practice and develop character forming habits during the school day. For example, students are explicitly taught and reminded that their teachers work very hard to help them be success-ful and therefore it is right to show gratitude. The routine to support this is that students say "thank you miss/sir" whenever they leave a lesson, or whenever they are helped by a member of staff. The power of this as a cultural norm means that whatever time in the year a student joins and no matter what habits they have, it becomes automatic very quickly. Another routine for developing gratitude is appreciations. Every day at lunch, stu-dents spend five minutes on their tables taking it in turn to express grati-tude to someone in the school community. The script for this is "I would like to give an appreciation to…for…I am grateful for this because…so two claps on the count of 2, 1-2." Three students are then selected each day to say these aloud to the rest of the year group. A third routine is postcards. At the end of each half term, students spend at least 30 minutes writ-ing thank you cards to at least two of their teachers. Teachers are trained on how to deliver these sessions and share model examples of thank you cards from previous half terms to support their tutees to write something heartfelt and specific.*

5 ***Constant Narration:*** *Examples of good character are shared by staff through the day on an instant messaging group called "Soane Shoutouts." This helps staff constantly reinforce this through line ups, tutor time and weekly assemblies where students are praised, rewarded and reminded of expectations. Tutors are also trained on how to celebrate examples of great character in order to normalise it and build a positive tutor group identity.*

6 ***Monitoring:*** *As with every aspect of the school, we regularly return to our list of traits to consider whether these truly are the things that characterise our students. We reflect on whether we need more focus from staff on a particular trait, more teaching, more narration to students, or more rou-tines and rituals to support students to develop good character.*

## Literacy and the curriculum

Clearly, if pupils cannot read, they cannot access a large swathe of the curriculum. Leaders will have had the common experience of pupils coming late to the UK and displaying phenomenal Maths skills unmatched by their inability to read even simple sentences in English. In the next chapter, we will explore what to do to support pupils who have English as an additional language.

The answer to pupils finding reading challenging is definitely not to give them extra English lessons: our ability to read is underpinned by broad knowledge across a range of areas, so pupils need to be reading History texts in History, Science texts in Science, and so on. It is also not to teach reading skills, which are without much evidence of impact.[5]

## How much are they reading?

In a secondary school, the best way to develop pupil literacy is to ensure that they are reading a lot, across the curriculum. I would mandate a minimum of one side of A4 for pupils to read per lesson of subject-specific text, and I would do that in almost all subjects. The exceptions? PE, unless you have enough time to practise as well as read. Some lessons might be fully practical, and that is ok. Maths: while I'd script explanations in a textbook, pupils mainly need to do a lot of Maths problems to get better at Maths. And in languages, clearly an entire page of French will be overwhelming for novices; that's not to say they can't read instructions and explanations, however.

Ideally, pupils also have 20 to 30 minutes a day of reading aloud with their form tutor or a reading teacher, simply reading a novel that is well chosen for their age and ability, to normalise reading for enjoyment. I say reading aloud, because for pupils who find reading tough, giving them time to silently read is basically giving them time to daydream. They simply won't do it.

## Helping pupils get better at reading

There will be pupils who cannot read, and these pupils – who I suspect will be an increasingly shrinking number given the improvements in primary phonics checks – will require a robust phonics programme delivered by a trained expert.

You could use reading age tests to determine pupils progress, though these give a false sense of specificity to educators. I've had pupils jump seven years in one, apparently, or regress when I can hear with my ears how much better their reading is. A reading age test will give you a decent indication across a cohort whether what you are doing is working or not, but for pupil-level data, I've found them to be spurious (perhaps improvements have occurred in recent years that makes this suggestion unfair).

The way you get better at something is to be guided to entry level, so you can access it, and then a lot of deliberate practice – that is, reading a lot. The more your curriculum requires reading across subjects, the more your pupils read each day, the better at reading they will become. It is a little like magic, because you don't really need to worry too much about it if the curriculum is set up well. Of course, setting up a curriculum rich in literacy is no easy object.

## Literacy expectations across departments

Like anything in schools, it can be easier to mandate something across the board and to row back later or through follow-up one-to-ones. If you work with all middle leaders on the importance of literacy and your curriculum expectations, it is easier to then take the Head of Maths aside and say: look, about that – here's what we expect of your department. In one school, I worked with HoDs one by one to increase the amount of reading in their subject, and I had pushback from every single subject except English: everyone had a reason that reading shouldn't be prioritised in their subject. It is true, you are not being tested on your ability to read about Art in a GCSE Art exam; it is also true that pupils at A-level Art struggle with the more academic artist study aspect; it is also true that the more pupils know about Art and its techniques and key figures, the more artistically literate they will be and the better able they will be to be creative in the Art space. Think of Art as part Art, part History of Art. Most Art teachers are actually quite excited about this possibility in the end.

And, indeed, there is a balance to be struck: leaders must also respect the centrality of the subject, and subject leaders are likely to understand the needs and demands of their subject with significantly more nuance and detail. When determining the extent to which literacy should underpin the subjects you manage, aim to research what the best schools are doing – the schools which are supporting pupils overall to develop their literacy as well as ensuring they achieve exceptional outcomes – and be guided by them as well as your in-house middle leaders.

---

**Stuart Morton, Vice Principal at Orchard Mead Academy in Leicester, writes about investing in literacy as a whole school**

*After completing reading assessments for the entire secondary cohort, we put together a six month plan for training, grouping and executing a plan to become a "Reading school" after realising that reading was possibly the number one reason why attainment, engagement and, to some extent, behaviour wasn't where we wanted it to be.*

*Together with the Head of English, the special educational needs co-ordinator (SENCO) and the educational psychologist, we committed to a training programme that covered all the way from phonics up to expert readers and everything in between. We made videos to share online with staff and created evaluations to establish staff understanding and launched the programme in September 2020.*

*We created reading coaches and committed huge amounts of money, including some from grants, to buying books and stocking the library. We made reading a standing item on all staff professional development delivery and made sure we explicitly modelled reading lessons with teachers so they could experience expert modelling of how it feels academically and emotionally.*

*We timetabled a reading lesson every day and tested the reading levels of pupils every three months to ensure progress was constant. We had authors come to visit and enrolled the local universities to invest in resources and offer days on campus.*

*The initiatives had multiple benefits, including moving from 45% of children meeting their chronological reading age to 75% and making 2 months progress for each month during our work.*

## Exam year groups

It is hard to know where "raising attainment" sits in the scope of this book – clearly, this is something secondary senior leaders think hard about and spend a lot of time on. I've settled for this chapter, though the reality is that your approach to working with exam groups will encompass their behaviour and motivation, the teaching they experience as well as the operational factors like their exam timetables and when they may (or may not) undertake additional interventions.

Ultimately, exam year groups will always be a balancing act for any leader. Spend too much time raising attainment in year 6, 11, or 13 and you risk results dipping for those in years 4, 7, and 10 when they finally come through. Put all your "best" teachers on Year 11, you fail to develop your teaching team to manage pupil progress in the long term.

At the same time, particularly for schools that have challenging results or that are seeking to rapidly turn around to attract more pupil applications, it would be remiss to not have a focused plan to ensure that pupils getting ready for national exams are in the strongest possible position they can be in.

---

### David Thomas, a senior leader across two multi-academy trusts, shares an approach crafted in 2022 about how leaders might go about raising attainment in year 11

*Raising achievement is about getting the simple things right, in detail, to the last child, every day of the year.*

#### Year 10 mocks

Run a mock exam series

*In the summer term of Year 10, students should do a set of mock exams. These should be as close to real exams as is possible given where students are in the course. At least core subjects should be taken in the exam hall in formal exam conditions so that students start acclimatising to these. Ideally, give students timetables in the same format as exam timetables, including seating plans.*

### Centrally analyse Year 10 mock results

*Here are some crucial bits of analysis to do:*

- **Headline results**. *This should include: Basics and EBacc at 4+, 5+ and 7+; Progress 8 overall and by bucket; Attainment 8 overall and by bucket; all of the above by PP and SEND. Compare these to your targets to see what needs to be achieved over the next year. Following the basics of this playbook should see an increase of at least 1.5 grades on average between end of Year 10 and real exams*

- **Subject results**. *This should include the full grade distribution and an estimate of progress*

- **Crossover analysis**. *This means creating a table with English grades as one axis and Maths grades as the other. Students are put into a cell based on their mock exam performance. Use this to work out target groups:*

  - *Students with 4+ in both should progress to 5+ in both, but need to have an eye kept on them*

  - *Students with 4+ in one and 3+ in the other should all make it to 5+ in both with the right support, and will need an individual plan to make sure this is in place*

  - *Students with 3+ in both can make it to 5+ with the right support and motivation. You should target at least two thirds of these students making it. They will need an individual plan, and a named adult responsible for shepherding them through the year*

  - *There will be students with lower grades who can make it to 5+ where there are particular circumstances. They'll need the same support as the 3+ target students*

  - *Treat Us on Higher Maths as a Grade 3, unless you have a reason to do otherwise*

- **Progress analysis**. *Rank students by an estimate of their individual P8 contribution (e.g. Subject Progress Index [SPI] in SISRA). You would expect that following this playbook adds 1.5 onto the current position. Look at any student who is below -2 (implying you'd expect them to be below -0.5 next summer). These are your target students for progress, and will need individualised support to bring them up to at least 0 by next summer.*

*Make important decisions based on results*

*Once you've done your analysis, there are a set of early decisions to make:*

■ **Target students** – *You need to decide your groups of target students and who falls into each group. You need to decide how you will communicate this to staff in a memorable way. Some will be targets for crossover, some for progress, some for both. Each target student will go on a spreadsheet where you track what support is in place for them*

■ **Subject line management** – *Where there are concerns about progress or attainment in a particular subject you may need to change the line management of that subject. If there is a subject where you are expecting progress to be below 0.5 then ensure there is a strong SLT line manager. That member of SLT will need to learn the exam spec and conduct a thorough review with the HoD before the end of the summer term to agree actions for next year*

■ **Tiers** – *In tiered subjects (Maths, Science, Modern Foreign Languages [MFLs]) you may need to move students between tiers. As a rule of thumb, MFL tiers can be changed in Year 11 but Maths and Science can't. We don't leave students in Higher "just in case" in Maths and Science. If a student is getting a 3 or low 4 in Maths on Higher, then they should move to Foundation. If they're getting below a 4-4 in Combined Science they should move to Foundation. If a student is getting below a 6-6-5 in separate Sciences, you should consider moving to Combined.*

*Run subject meetings to go through results and actions*

*Every exam subject should have a meeting to go through results. This meeting should include the SLT member in charge of raising achievement, the Head of Department, and the SLT line manager for that subject. The Principal and Head of Year should also be present whenever possible (at a minimum, for English, Maths and Science). The meeting should be owned by the Head of Department, and treated as their opportunity to share their subject's status with SLT. It should cover, at a minimum:*

1  *Headline results*

2  *Disadvantaged group results (PP and SEND at a minimum)*

3  *Strengths and weaknesses from the mock exams (to the level of specific topics or questions where students were strong/weak)*

4  *Specific students of concern*

5  *Actions the Head of Department is planning to take based on all of the above*

6  *Requests the Head of Department has for SLT based on all of the above*

*Communicate results and actions back to students and parents*

*Plan the communication of results carefully. Ensure that teachers do not give results back in a trickle to students in class. Instead, produce a formal results sheet that you will give to students in a planned way – for example at the end of an end of day assembly with the Principal and Head of Year. Where you have already got an action plan in place, share these actions so that students know what support they are getting*

## Planning for Year 11

*You need to finish the summer term with a comprehensive plan for how Year 11s will be supported in the autumn. Ideally, this should all be communicated to students and parents before the end of the year.*

### Make the most of the time you already have

*The best resource you have for raising achievement is lessons. You need to get the most out of these – no intervention can make up for poor teaching during Year 11. Here are some of the things to consider:*

1 **Teacher placement** – *Which classes are your target students in? Are the strongest teachers taking those classes? Are there any absence risks on classes with target students? If so, what is your back-up plan should absence hit during the year?*

2 **Curriculum plan** – *Does the Year 11 curriculum for each subject match up with the strengths and weaknesses discussed in the subject improvement meeting? Is it well-enough tailored to the exam students are taking? Things to check include: does the balance of time in the plan match the weighting of components; are exam questions/components taught explicitly rather than just content being taught; is any coursework finished early enough in the year to not crossover with exam revision?*

3 **Homework plan** – *Is there a homework plan that covers the whole year? Is it demanding enough, and does it include enough exam practice? In both English and Maths, a minimum would be a set of homework on content and a timed past exam paper per week. Remember that the Department for Education expect Year 11s to be doing 2-2.5 hours of extra study per day. If yours are doing less, they will do less well in the exams than their peers elsewhere in the country. How is homework being monitored? Will the Head of Year and Raising Attainment lead know on the same day if a child misses their Maths paper?*

4 **Exam preparation** – *Is there a clear plan covering the year for how students will be ready for exams? This should include when each available past paper is being done, when walking talking mocks are scheduled, how*

*students are getting enough practice of timed exam questions (especially extended writing ones)*

### Make more time

*The best schools in the country are adding significant amounts of teaching time. There are trusts who run a 28 lesson week for Years 7-11 – which means their children have had 111 extra school days by the end of Year 11. The most advantaged children are getting private tutors outside of school. We owe it to our children to give them more time with expert teachers so that they can do well.*

*Extra teaching time is best when it is in a student's normal class group, with their normal teacher. It feels more like a normal lesson, and is taught by a teacher who knows exactly what they need to learn. This should always be the goal. Where this isn't possible, think carefully about arrangements so that you are getting the most out of the time.*

*Options for more time include the following:*

1 **Form time** *– You can use this in a number of ways. Be careful to ensure that this does not disrupt your plan for supporting students with post-16 or with pastoral care. Options include:*

   a *Turn it into a timetabled lesson*

   b *Allocate students to new form groups for Year 11 based on their target subjects (e.g. put students in your English 5+ target group with an English teacher as their form tutor) and practice this subject in form time*

   c *Run quizzing and revision – for example, you could bring Year 11 into the hall for English Literature content quizzing, or split them between two spaces for Higher and Foundation Science quizzing*

2 **After school** *– We pay staff to teach after school or include it in their timetabled hours if they are under allocation. As a default, you should expect all of Year 11 to be staying for a timetabled additional lesson on four days a week. This must be timetabled and treated as a lesson – it is not an optional extra or a session with lower expectations. Treat students well, for example by giving them a drink and a snack at the end of the regular school day or when they finish this extra lesson*

3 Saturday/holiday schools *– We pay staff to teach these. Select subjects where you know extra work is going to be required to hit targets, and focus resources on these. A default Saturday school would be 9:30-12, with pizza served at midday as a reward*

*Focus extra support at target students*

Students in target groups will need extra support. Options include:

1 **Residentials** – *Target students who need support to study effectively during the holiday, or who need a morale boost, can be taken away for residentials. If doing as an early morale boost to get investment into the Year 11 journey, do this early in the year. If doing as study support, do this in February half-term. A default would be 3 days, two nights, with a mixture of taught revision sessions and team-building activities*

2 **Mentoring** – *Every child who needs to make significant progress in Year 11 needs a named adult looking after them. Get staff to volunteer to do this, especially non-teaching staff (who can often be the most effective mentors). Mentoring should be weekly, and can be done 1-1 or in a small group. You could consider running mentoring as a breakfast before school, where pastries and drinks are provided. Mentoring works best if mentors are given a schedule of discussion topics so that each session is focused (e.g. drawing up a shortlist of post-16 courses to apply to, reviewing homework from last week).*

*Plan the motivational journey as well as the academic one*

Year 11 is an emotional journey as much as it is an intellectual one. Have a plan in advance for how you will motivate students through the year. Possible entrants into the plan include:

1 **Assemblies** – *Have a schedule in advance, including special guest assemblies and assemblies on particular messages from the Principal. Think about the critical times (e.g. the run up to mock exams) and make sure you are in control of the message. Have some contingency assemblies ready to deploy when common problems bubble (e.g. an assembly on stress, one on not falling out with each other).*

2 **Careers** – *Get everyone's applications for post-16 done by the end of January. It makes a world of difference knowing that is all sorted.*

3 **Treats** – *Work hard play hard. Consider surprise treats when they've just been great (why not give every Year 11 a Fab on the way out of school on Friday if they've been Fab that week?). Recognise their efforts at the end of mock exams (hire in a couple of bouncy castles, take them bowling). Remember that surprise gestures of appreciation mean more than "if you do this then we'll give you" rewards.*

4 **Wellbeing** – *Some students will find Year 11 difficult. Consider some structured de-stressing options for them, such as morning mindfulness, a yoga club, Y11 Friday football.*

*Stay on top of your target students*

*Once you have your Year 11 plan, create a spreadsheet that maps your target students against the support in place. Go through row by row and check that the support matches the scale of the task. You then need a plan for keeping on top of these students during the year. The biggest risks are poor attendance and poor behaviour. Pre-empt these by:*

1 ***Meeting with students and parents*** *– Where you know there is an attendance or behaviour risk, meet to discuss your plan for next year. Do this positively – have an "Academic Support" meeting not an "Attendance Improvement" meeting. Students are often ready to make a transition into Year 11 where they want to do well. Capitalise on this. Use the meeting to show what the school will do to support, and get commitments from the student/parent about what they will do (e.g. what is their plan if X is unwell, or feeling like he/she doesn't want to come to school).*

2 ***Have a rapid action safety net ready to deploy*** *– Make sure your attendance officer knows who your target students are. If one isn't in school, they need to be the first phone call. Know who will be going to knock on their door if they're not in school quickly. Similarly, make sure your behaviour team know who your target students are. If one ends up withdrawn from lesson then have a plan for getting them the work ASAP and having a leader drop in to work through what went wrong.*

*Communicate your plan with students and parents*

*Every child is lucky to have a school that is putting in place a plan like this to give them the best possible chance of success. Make them feel that. Tell parents how many extra hours of support their child is getting, and the monetary value of that. Tell students how lucky they are that their teachers are putting in extra for them. Make them feel like the luckiest children on the planet.*

## Start of Year 11

*The focus here should be on hitting the ground running with pace and a sense of urgency. Make sure your plan is happening in the first couple of weeks – if the start goes well it is easy to keep momentum. Specific things to do in the first few weeks include the following:*

1 ***Raising achievement evening for parents*** *– Bring all Year 11 parents in for a short evening where you talk them through how Year 11 works and what they can do to support their child. The most important thing for parents is to make sure their child gets at least 8 hours of sleep a night. The second most important thing is to make sure they are doing at least 2 hours of study a day*

2 ***Check in on actions and requests from the summer term*** – *Make sure that all the actions Heads of Department committed to in the summer term meetings have happened. Make sure that requests have been either granted and acted on or that the Head of Department has been given a reason why it can't happen and offered an alternative*

3 ***Explicitly teach how to revise*** – *You should do a generic session, perhaps in an assembly, on the science of learning and what effective revision is (quizzing/past papers) and isn't (re reading study guides). Subject teachers should explicitly teach how to revise in their subject. You should offer a series of "guided revision" sessions after-school, where Heads of Department model how to do half an hour of revision in their subject, just as they would recommend students do it at home*

4 ***Check in with students*** – *Run at least one focus group of Year 11s to find out how they're feeling, and get any early feedback on unintended consequences/miscommunications*

## November mock exams

*These have two purposes: to give you accurate data about where students are at, and to get them familiar with what their exams will feel like.*

### Set the right exam papers

*Heads of Department will need to set exam papers. You need to check that they are either (a) a full past exam series or (b) as close to this as possible. There will be reasons why (a) is not possible in some subjects, for example you wouldn't sit a history paper on a period you haven't studied yet. However, you would sit a full maths series, even if there are a couple of topics left to study. As senior leaders you need to check that the papers are going to give you an accurate picture of where students are at. Ask how much of the course these papers cover, whether they cover all assessment objectives fully, whether this paper tends to be easier or harder than another omitted paper, etc.*

*At this stage you should also agree grade boundaries. If they are past exam series you should use the real boundaries plus a buffer (usually 5% as a rule of thumb, but depends on the subject). If they are not then you should use the past exam series as a starting point.*

*All of this should be done before the October half-term. It is also worth making sure that Heads of Department physically check the papers once printed so that there are no photocopying issues that rear their head in the mocks and so invalidate data.*

### Decide how to weight non-exam elements

*For subjects with non-exam components (e.g. GCSE Music) you should decide in advance how you will include the non-exam components in the mock grades. The ideal is as close to possible as the actual GCSE. You don't want to have mock grades that are just the exam paper when this isn't how the actual GCSE is determined.*

### Prepare students in exam technique

*Dedicate some time in advance of mock exams to making sure students know how to tackle the exam papers. You do not want to have data that is artificially low because students didn't know how to approach the papers. In English and Maths you should run at least one walking talking mock in each subject before the mock exams.*

### Mimic real exams as closely as possible

*Do this by:*

- *Giving exam timetables in the same format as normal*

- *Having an exam seating plan*

- *Lining up by row in advance*

- *Checking equipment is in clear pencil cases, no bottles with labels, etc.*

- *Giving the same JCQ (Joint Council for Qualifications) regulations exam announcement as you would in a real exam*

- *Using external invigilators and barring teachers from the hall*

- *Doing the same encouragement and psyching up that you will in the summer*

### Analyse results and take action

*Complete the same analysis as in the Year 10 mock section above, and hold subject meetings in the same way. After this, adjust your intervention plan accordingly (considering all the same options for intervention as in the section above).*

### Have some fun after the exams

*Show the students that you care about them, not just their results, by organising a way for them to let their hair down at the end of the mocks. Do whatever will work best in your context. I have done: going to the trampoline park, going bowling, putting bouncy castles on the field, offering a choice of smaller (more-chilled) things for an afternoon.*

### Run a mock results evening

*Teachers should not give grades back to students in class. They can give papers back if helpful for teaching, but grades should be kept confidential. Release these via a results print out (the same as they'd get in the summer) that are collected in envelopes at a mock results evening. This should be attended by parents – you may wish to say that only a parent can collect the results. At this evening you should do a presentation to parents and students on how to respond to results, and launch your plan for Christmas revision. You should come into this evening with a list of parents you need to speak to, and have allocated staff to pick out those parents and have the required conversations.*

### Prepare for Christmas revision

*Get students to plan for their holiday revision under supervision. Give them a template timetable, with clear guidance on how much they should be doing each day and how many days they should be working. Subjects should give clear guidance on what activities to do and how to chunk the revision up. A bad revision timetable would just be a list of subject names in time slots. A good one is which activities are being done in each time slot (e.g. "Write one timed Romeo and Juliet essay from the revision guide, chosen at random by my mum"). Send these completed timetables to parents as well as letting students take them home.*

## February/March mock exams

*Follow the same steps as for the November mocks in the above section (with Easter revision instead of Christmas revision), plus:*

### February half-term residential

*Take target students away for two days during the February half-term as a residential trip. This should be half English/Maths teaching, and half activities (e.g. outdoor teambuilding). The purpose is to make sure (a) that they spend half-term doing productive revision and (b) that they feel special.*

## Preparing for, and doing, the real exams

### Coursework/non exam assessment

*All coursework should be finished and submitted by Christmas of Year 11, with the exception of the final section of GCSE art portfolios (that build up to the examined piece).*

### Planning guided/taught revision

*It is important to meticulously timetable the exam period and the immediate run-up to it. There should be one central timetable of all guided revision sessions – otherwise departments end up competing for students and running clashing sessions. This central timetable should work back from when the exams are held, and should include:*

- Collapsed lessons in the school day, when students leave their normal timetabled lesson to join a revision activity (e.g. walking talking mock before English and Maths exams)

- After school revision sessions, which should be offered on the evening before major exams (with catering provided, e.g. takeaway pizza)

- Saturday schools, which should be offered for core subjects during the summer term (again, with catering provided)

This timetable should be shared with students in the first week back after the Easter holiday so that they can plan what they are attending. It is essential that target students meet with a member of staff, preferably with their parents in attendance, to agree what they will attend.

### Designing revision plans

There should be a whole-school approach to designing revision plans. This means having:

- **Department-designed revision activities** – Students should have a menu of revision activities provided by the department, so that they do not have to prepare their own activities.

- **Centrally designed revision timetable** – This should be a paper pack of week timetables, where students can write in which activities from the department guides they are going to do in which time slots

These plans should be completed under staff supervision. Target students should have a mentor go through their plan with them, and hold them to account for completing it.

### Prom points

If you have an end of Year 11 celebration (probably called a prom), then make sure there is a system of reward points to earn a discounted ticket for attending/completing revision activities.

### Exam routine/ritual

It is important to make sure that the routine for going into and sitting exams is as calming and consistent as possible. Think carefully about the physical spaces – how do they look, are they decorated well, are there motivational messages from their teachers on the wall? Think carefully about reducing extra things to remember – give students the same seat for every exam so they don't have to remember different seat numbers, have a system for depositing mobile phones securely. Think carefully about setting the right tone – have bananas or similar snacks available for anyone with flagging *energy levels, make it easy to fill up water bottles or have bottled water on hand.*

*Think carefully about the ritual – how do students go in to the exam? There should be a pep talk from the head of department for that subject before each exam, or from another senior leader if they are not available. Totteridge Academy have a "haka" they perform before going into the hall. Think about what will boost mood and confidence that works for your school culture. Also think carefully about what happens after an exam. Do students go straight back to lessons, or do they get a breaktime to debrief? How long will it last? Who supervises it? There should be a senior leader on hand at the end of every exam in case students are upset or need support.*

### Study leave

*This should not be granted other than to Year 13.*

### Lessons during the exam period

*Have a clear school expectation for how lessons are conducted during the exam period. Every lesson should either be taught as normal (e.g. if the exams for that subject have not all happened yet), or should be silent revision (e.g. if exams for that subject have all happened). This will require clear school expectations about student preparation for revision (e.g. they will need revision materials with them).*

### End of school attendance

*Have a clear process for how and when the school year ends, and set this out at Easter. This should include being clear on when students' last lesson is (e.g. will they go home at lunchtime if their last exam is in the morning?). There should be a process for being signed out and no longer having to attend, including having staff confirm that no materials are due for return (e.g. no library books, no subject equipment). This process should also include collecting information on students' planned destinations (even if already collected, just to confirm).*

## Early years

The Early Years of school are something of a beast unto themselves. Although by the end of Reception, an Early Years space can start to resemble a "regular" classroom, that is certainly not how three- and four-year-olds begin their school journey. I certainly found it a challenge as a secondary trained leader to wrap my head around why Early Years looked so different from other parts of the school.

Children in their earliest stages of schooling are learning, almost by necessity, in a different way. One past colleague spoke to me about how to consider this, noting that the children in Reception were closer to being babies than to sitting their SATs, and rather than imagining how to get them to the point where they could sit at desks and read and write for hours, I should instead consider how you get a toddler to be able to sit for any length of time and focus.

Children in Early Years benefit from continuous provision, which largely looks like learning through well-set-up play activities. During these activities, professionals work on extending their play and supporting young people to work together. There are, of course, teacher-led elements, such as story time, circle time, and phonics input, but these tend to be brief. Over the course of Early Years, the time spent with the input of the teacher or an extended activity builds up, and in the best Early Years settings, you see children beginning to write independently, sitting at desks, for short bursts (and often in the morning).

---

### Maria Craster, Assistant Principal at One Degree Academy in London, shares her approach to the leadership of Early Years

*The Early Years and Foundation stage is a magical and unique phase in our education system. Practitioners are encouraged to focus on the unique child, exploring both biologically primary (things we are evolved to learn, like communicating our needs and walking) and biologically secondary (things we need to be explicitly taught, like reading or counting) learning. The rate at which young people develop and change astounds me every year and is a big part of the reason I am still working in this phase 8 years later.*

*At One Degree, our vision is to give all children a life of choice and opportunity, regardless of the starting point; this starts from their very first day with us. We know that a big struggle of working in EYFS (early years foundation stage) is achieving the right balance between adult-directed and child-led learning: children are unlikely to learn to have back and forth conversations during a carpet session. Equally, they will not learn to read through independent play. That balance is something that we have worked hard to get right. My key takeaway has been that every child and every cohort is different, and that the need to be reflective and adaptive is paramount.*

*A focus of my leadership this year has been how we translate our successful model from being a one form entry Reception (28 students and 2 members of staff) to now, when we are considerably larger and still growing (91 students and 10 members of staff). I found it much easier to translate the structured elements of the day into a "Blueprint" for staff to follow: they have clear guidelines for most key routines to make it easier to ensure consistency and enable practitioners to focus on the important act of building relationships and delivering great teaching, and not spending their time thinking about the structure of the day and transitional activities. We review, tweak and* improve these systems each year, but having this consistent starting point has really reduced the workload for both myself and colleagues. Examples of this include what the "soft start" progression looks like in each term, how to run lunchtime and the structure of our Phase 1 Phonics sessions.

What's great now is that our vision of good practice in Early Years is established well enough and consistently across the team that they know what is fixed and can't be altered, but they also have the knowledge and the skills to know what can be adapted to suit each cohort and unique child and personalize it. For example, the curriculum maps provide ideas of role play ideas that provide a range of opportunities for children to develop across the curriculum, however, teachers are free to follow their cohort's interests and implement their own ideas if they prefer. This model allows support for our less experienced teachers but provides flexibility for those who are more experienced and have their own amazing ideas.

Ensuring quality teaching and provision was a less straightforward problem: it has been paramount to ensure consistency and shared vision. We have adapted our training cycle so that the whole team meets every Monday after school (teachers and teaching assistants). In these sessions we read from recent, relevant EYFS pedagogy, watch videos and reflect on our own setting as well as sharing best practice we might have seen elsewhere. This collaborative approach ensures that every member of the team's voice is heard and a shared understanding and language is created.

For me, the most important skill of an EYFS practitioner is the ability to play and use play powerfully to push learning on. We have looked at key educational approaches, such as Rosenshine,[6] and thought about how these apply to EYFS. How can retrieval practice take place in the sand tray? How can you use scaffolds and gradually reduce them when playing in the construction area? In our training sessions we rehearse quality adult-child interactions with a big focus on talk. We model great vocabulary and give children opportunities to apply this in play in a way that is purposeful to them. I then ensure that I am in class modelling this and providing feedback to staff on both play as well as their directed teaching as we know what we make important, is important.

We don't take a top-down approach at One Degree Academy. Instead, we look at where we can draw parallels. In our training sessions we rehearse quality adult-child interactions with a big focus on talk. We model great vocabulary and give children opportunities to apply this in play in a way that is purposeful to them. I then ensure that I am in class modelling this and providing feedback to staff on both play as well as their directed teaching as we know what we make important, is important.

Our EYFS is constantly changing and this is thanks to the fabulous team that I am lucky enough to work with. They know and share in the vision and I'm excited to see where we will take it next.

# Sixth form

At the other end of the schooling spectrum are the final two years of sixth form. In the UK, this looks very different from what has gone before. Pupils have chosen the subjects they want to study and they take these subjects for many more hours than they have previously. They then have significant amounts of study time in between those subjects.

The curriculum for sixth form subjects must therefore be carefully considered. Not only must pupils cover the curriculum and prepare for an exam in a far shorter time than they have had in the secondary school run-up to GCSEs, they must also be guided as to how to use their study time wisely. There is a balance to be struck: if you set, say, six hours of homework, teachers will feel the burden of having to give feedback on all of that work. If you set pure "self-directed study" or "lesson preparation", it is unlikely the pupils will do it. (I say this based more on my own experiences rather than on the black box of what our children do when they leave school: as someone who had the good fortune to win a free place at a private school, I will say that during my sixth form experience there, none of my peers nor I bothered doing the set pre-reading, much as we loved the subjects we had chosen and privileged as we undoubtedly were.)

I would be opting for pen to paper when setting independent study: summarise Chapters 2 to 6, for example, that teachers can simply check by sight. Of course, pupils will need to write at length independently, and you can gauge the extent to which they are able to do this at home, and perhaps at the start you can give them 30 minutes to make a decent start of it in the lesson with your direct support. (Ask them to rule off with a red pen where they got to in the lesson so you can check that they have truly added to their work independently.)

In my experience, the aspect that teachers find most challenging when teaching sixth form is their subject and curriculum knowledge. Advising, or even mandating, that teachers become exam markers during the summer term (and, if you can, freeing them up to do this work) can go some way towards building their curriculum expertise. It is unlikely that you will have the willing team or the time available to have all teachers do this, but explicitly asking those who do to present on their work can be helpful to others in the department. Ensuring that HoDs set aside ample time for subject and curriculum knowledge development is also key: HoDs might need to pivot from rehearsal of pedagogy techniques to reading and discussing high-level texts or concepts and rehearsing explanations and practising questioning.

Lesson planning for sixth form lessons is often more of a challenge for teachers: the classes tend to be smaller and the subject matter more complex; there is more time for teaching and less time behaviour managing, so pupils get through much more material. This all sounds great, but if teachers spend 8/10 of their time planning their non-sixth form lessons, this can feel out of sync and tougher to execute. Again, support your HoDs to run expert planning sessions.

**Patrick Farmborough, Assistant Director of Education at the Greenshaw Learning Trust, explores the strategic aspects of running a successful Sixth Form**

*In my career, I've had the opportunity to work with a large number of Sixth Forms – initially as a Head of Sixth Form, then as a Headteacher, and finally as someone overseeing Sixth Forms across a large multi academy trust. Across the most successful of these Sixth Forms, I've seen a number of different approaches, but the most effective always include three vital pillars: A shared approach to the leadership of the Sixth Form, a deliberate and considered approach to students' independent study, and a constant focus on teachers' subject knowledge.*

### 1 *A Distributed Approach to Leadership*

*In too many schools, Sixth Form is often seen as slightly separate to the rest of the school. This is unsurprising: Sixth Forms are rarely urgent problems – behaviour is generally easier to manage than the rest of the school, and, having chosen to stay, students and parents are generally much happier with the status quo. The problem is that this deprives the Sixth Form of a huge wealth of leadership expertise and capacity. When the Head of Sixth Form is responsible for everything – behaviour, teaching and learning, enrichment and so on – even the most exceptional leader will be unable to lead all of these well.*

*By contrast, in the highest performing Sixth Forms, the whole school feels invested in the Sixth Form. This starts with the Headteacher. They talk about Year 13 at least as much as Year 11 – probably more. The Teaching and Learning lead always makes sure CPD is relevant to Sixth Form teaching. The Behaviour Lead ensures that school policies and procedures apply to the Sixth Form. Middle Leaders are just as on top of their A Level groups as any other. This is not to say that things will be exactly the same in Year 12 and 13 as the rest of the school; they won't. But these differences will be carefully and proactively planned for.*

*The Head of Sixth Form's role shifts from trying to lead everything themselves to holding the rest of the SLT to account for their remits within the Sixth Form – along with the various elements of Sixth Form which fall outside this (e.g. Universities and Colleges Admissions Service [UCAS]).*

### 2 *A Deliberate Approach to Independent Study*

*Perhaps the biggest difference in Sixth Form is the importance of independent study. As a rough guide, the best schools set at least an hour of independent study for every taught hour. This might seem like a lot – but if the average school provides five hours of teaching per week in each A Level, this still only adds up to 15 hours of lessons and 15 hours of independent study.*

*This can be a difficult change for both staff and students. Teachers are not used to setting such a high volume of independent work, and often overlook this in their planning. Students are not used to having to organise and self-direct so much of their time.*

*The best Sixth Forms plan for this deliberately. Staff are expected to think carefully about independent work: curriculum plans should clearly set out what independent work will be set. Generic revision tasks should be avoided. There should be clear processes to check it is completed, and that the quality is sufficient – and, yes, there should be clear sanctions for non-completion.*

*Students are similarly supported. Most high-performing Sixth Forms keep students on site for the whole school day, insisting that students spend their free periods in independent study. In the best examples, these periods are staffed by experts who can support students with learning. Students are deliberately and explicitly taught study skills and expected to demonstrate them regularly. Staff are clear what work has been set for each student in each subject and ensure that students use their time wisely. As a result, students are considerably less dependent on home study – which we know can be particularly challenging for more disadvantaged groups.*

### 3 *A relentless focus on Subject Knowledge*

*A common question is what distinguishes Sixth Form teaching from the rest of the school. Again, I have heard a variety of answers, but the one thing which came up in every high performing Sixth Form was subject knowledge. Teaching students to A\* standard in an A Level requires teachers to have subject knowledge well beyond this standard.*

*The best schools invest heavily in supporting their teachers in building subject knowledge through building a culture of scholarship amongst staff as well as students. They prioritise regular, subject-specific CPD, encouraging and supporting staff to become examiners, and engagement with wider networks outside of school. The curriculum is ambitious, with students often pushed to move beyond core content and delve into greater level detail. Staff very carefully consider exactly how they will teach the more challenging topics, and exactly what tasks will support students in consolidating this knowledge. Lessons constantly refer to exemplar materials and success criteria to ensure students have a detailed understanding of what the top grades look like, and students are given regular opportunities to practice and receive feedback.*

## Hannah Turner, a Trust director of sixth form in Kent, explores some of the facets of running a successful sixth form

*If your Sixth Form is within a school, there needs to be recognition that sixth form works at a different pace to the rest of the school. There are certain aspects of sixth form leadership that are unique and often very few people within a school fully understand the role and responsibilities of a sixth form leader.*

*A leader of a sixth form prioritises their work according to the requirements of each term. Student recruitment, retention, progress, assessment and reporting, destinations (UCAS), careers, PSHE and personal development are consistent through the year, however there are times in which these aspects are heightened and require focus, and so the first step is to map your year and set termly priorities that incorporate all of these elements but also retain scope for further depth of work in key areas that are needed at that particular time of the year.*

*An example might be making sure that all promotional materials for your provision are up to date and accurate by the end of an academic year or the beginning of autumn term one ready for open evening in term two. Another example is sharing the academic bursary application process to parents and students in term 1 with reminders throughout the year.*

*In terms of recruiting to your sixth form, find opportunities across all key stages to promote the sixth form. Develop a student leadership team who will lead on this. Have frequent assembly slots and make sure that your open evening event is well planned and involves the work of the subject leaders and students. It is also important to ensure that you have access to year 11 students for taster days, preferably in term 2 and the run up to recruitment closing.*

*Ensure that the sixth form is involved in year 11 mock exams, whether that be in providing revision opportunities for students or in the provision of careers assemblies. Make sure that your application systems are tested before releasing them to parents and students. Create a culture in which sixth form recruitment is the responsibility of all colleagues, particularly subject leaders, by involving them in each step of the process including interviews, providing personalised offers to each student and eventually enrolment.*

*You might ask KS4 teachers to select students who may not have applied and send personalised "we want you" cards stating specific reasons why you want the student to consider sixth form. Ideally, send the cards to both students and parents as this can be extremely powerful. If your offer includes extracurricular provision, invite prospective students to train with or participate in the offer.*

*Opportunities to engage with sixth form students is key. The students in your sixth form are your most valuable asset and having a culture that promotes the sense of legacy and responsibility is fundamental in achieving success in recruitment. Over-communicating to prospective students that current students cannot wait to work with and welcome them to the community is fundamental to this approach.*

*Consider scheduling your work experience in term 3 of year 12 or any time other than term 6. This will enable you to access more varied opportunities than in the often-busier times of term 5 and 6 when other schools are looking to secure placements for year 10 and year 12 students. Encourage all students to find their own work experience places and support them with mock interviews, applications and CV support during tutor time and assembly time. Offer drop ins and additional school sessions where needed.*

*Use term four to term six for futures planning for year 12 where possible and commence UCAS work within this time too. Invite alumni in to give talks to students about their destination process and experiences and ask them to help you in creating useful up to date resources on finance, accommodation, assessment and university life ... particularly if it has been a while since you graduated, as the Higher Education landscape changes rapidly. Publish all materials created to parents and carers and hold an information evening or event and record and send this to all parents who couldn't attend.*

*Design your personal development and enrichment opportunities based on clear measurable objectives. Do you want to encourage volunteering? If so, why? Clearly communicate your why to all stakeholders and design a way to measure the impact. If you are creating a student leadership team, why? What value will they bring and why do this? Again, communicate the why and ensure that you can easily measure the effectiveness and impact of your decision. Linking enrichment to the curriculum is always important, but do you also need to consider more engaging skills-based enrichment or residentials that enhance cultural capital? Again, consider the why, over communicate this and measure impact.*

*Consider student voice carefully. Identify what it is that you seek to discover and be brave in challenging yourself to explore areas in depth. Why complete student voice? What can you do in response to it? If for example, students request further information on a Relationships and Sex Education topic, how can you do this and what is the best way of delivering this information? Identifying the usefulness of your PHSE programme and whether it is reaching all students and impact is extremely useful in addition to curriculum and culture feedback.*

*A Sixth form's strength lies within its culture and ethos. If your ethos is different from the main school, great. Do your students know this? Why is it different? What does it communicate about your students and is it meaningful?*

*Making culture visible is challenging but there are simple ways achieve this. Use the language of your ethos in everything that you do whether this be in staff briefings, assemblies, letters home, your website and social media, student leadership apparel, sports kit, merchandise, SLT meetings and CPD.*

*Use student rewards to do this. If, for example dedication is part of your ethos create a dedication award. Use the word dedication in your communication to all stakeholders. Creating a sense of belonging within your culture can be achieved via rewards, recognition, and communication. Surprising students with a whole sixth form reward, whether this be taking them off timetable for an afternoon for an activity or simply providing hot chocolate or cakes, can do a lot for morale and belonging.*

*Community and teamwork between teachers and students can be visible in their relationships and the way in which they communicate with one another. Having colleagues share spaces with students at particular times in the year (assessments, feedback, futures preparation) can have significant impact. Culture can be a good starting point for all strategic decisions made within sixth form leadership. The diving question could be, does this align with our culture? Is this decision driven by culture?*

*Sixth form leaders have a complex and varied role. Key to understanding their role would be to spend time in the area and look at their termly objectives. There are great opportunities to work with sixth form leaders as part of the wider leadership team. They are often solitary leaders, constantly seeking further information on policy, funding, and census guidance. They can often be found with the exams officer or a subject leader. Mostly you will find them with students having in-depth conversations that pivot between subject content, challenging ideas and theories and excited conversations about the student's future.*

## Special educational needs and the curriculum

This part comes with a caveat that the guidance on the best curriculum for SEND pupils is not static. Professionals are being constantly updated on best practice insights by statutory regulations as well as accountability bodies, and in the duration of my career, this has changed significantly. I'll try to make it clear what are my own philosophy and experience and what is the current advice.

Firstly, to be clear, not all pupils with SEND need additional support in accessing the curriculum. There are SEND pupils who will be some of the highest-achieving you will ever teach. These children tend to not need any curriculum adaptations, and in the next chapter we'll explore the teaching adaptations you might make.

In most cases in mainstream schools, however, pupils with SEND achieve lower than their non-SEND counterparts; indeed, the Education Endowment Foundation (EEF) SEND report notes that "The attainment gap between pupils with SEND and their peers is twice as big as the gap between pupils eligible for free school meals and their peers," to contrast SEND with another chronically under-achieving cohort.[7] The curriculum can be one way to support SEND pupils to achieve more.

Put simply, if you have pupils who struggle to access learning, they are likely to move through the curriculum more slowly than their non-SEND counterparts. If we present the identical curriculum to all pupils regardless of their ability, we can feel like we have offered equality of access and equality of breadth in the curriculum. In some ways, this is definitely a good thing: overly restricting the curriculum, as we explored earlier, is counterproductive. Of course, there is a limit. If pupils are moving more slowly, we need to decrease either the breadth of their curriculum or the depth – there is no world in which they can move through the same material in the same time, and if they do, it is at the expense of achieving great outcomes that will set them up for future life success.

There are schools that make the blanket choice to remove some pupils from languages or arts subjects. I would urge caution in doing this too early. Particularly with languages, this is such a hierarchical curriculum that if you miss it for one year, you will need to be teaching that group again from point zero – they can't just join the others in their year group a year later.

Removing pupils from lessons for interventions on a carousel structure also has its challenges, particularly where middle leaders have carefully designed a curriculum that develops and builds knowledge incrementally. Pupils who miss one of their two or three lessons of a subject a week, particularly for a hierarchical subject like languages, can return to their next lesson even more out of their depth and present even more of a catch-up challenge for their teachers.

Unfortunately, it is not possible to have SEND pupils who are low-attaining study the full curriculum as well as benefit from bespoke interventions *and* achieve in line with their peers – or at least, I have yet to find a school that does this. Your best bet is to reduce the curriculum somewhere: either have pupils take one less lesson a week of a subject and deliver interventions in that "gained period" or reduce curriculum breadth across subjects so they are able to cover core material in depth – that is, have more time for the material they are studying. In either scenario, I'd recommend allocating your best teachers to these pupils, because if anyone is capable of helping them to make big gains, it is your best teachers. In my experience, investing in this in year 7 in a secondary school should help them to catch up most rapidly.

Having pupils with SEND be removed for interventions with non-teachers is not a strategy I would advocate: the children with the most complex challenges deserve and need to be taught by the best-qualified professionals. A far better method, which I've observed in just a few schools (which were all high-performing for pupils with SEND), is to train your teaching assistants to deliver parts of the curriculum to the pupils who most understand what is being taught, and have the teacher withdraw those who are finding the material challenging for short periods of the lesson. This group of pupils need not be the same every time: some pupils may be high-achieving in some parts of the curriculum and struggle with others; indeed, it is likely that most pupils are like this.

What is critical is not labelling children or assuming that they need something extra; what works best is teachers who identify the children who struggle and what they struggle with and schools that put systems in place to ensure that the children who struggle with that aspect can be taught it by an excellent, well-qualified teacher.

## Extra-curricular

I've long advocated that schools need to be expected to do less but expected to do what they do more effectively. The range of demands on schools is frankly ludicrous[8]; and all this when only half of secondary schools ensure that pupils leave with a strong pass in English and Maths.[9] If I'm being brutal, extra-curricular activities is on my long list of things schools could probably stop doing and have no negative impact on outcomes; indeed, it could even have a positive impact on outcomes, as you'd stop teachers doing something time-consuming and they could focus on either teaching their subject better or going home and getting some rest – which, I would argue, leads to their being able to teach better. (Happier, better-rested teachers are better able to respond to the changing needs of their class in real time; they are also less likely to become ill and be absent.)

Of course, not everyone agrees with me that outcomes are the ultimate aim of schooling, and that is why I'm including extra-curricular activities in this chapter on the curriculum: for many (most?) educators, a wide and varied experience of stuff that doesn't get tested is an essential part of schooling. Indeed, there is an argument to be made that much of the stuff that makes up cultural capital is found not in a classroom but in an art gallery and at the chess club. So there is a strong argument to be made for extra-curricular activities, which I respect and have carried out in the schools I have worked and led in.

In the best schools I have worked in, extra-curricular activities have been thoughtfully planned to complement a rigorously planned academic curriculum, and teachers have led these by choice and therefore with enthusiasm, but this, in my experience, is rare. If you have determined that an extra-curricular offer is important, asking for volunteers and hoping – particularly in a time of high teacher workloads – may not yield results. Adopting set parameters, such as that teachers need to run one club for one term in the academic year, or that every department must provide one or two extra-curricular offerings and then staff these reasonably, can help. Of course, if extra-curricular is core to your school, you might want to mandate that every member of staff run something. Building this into your timetable is one way to ensure it is done: teachers will see it as part of their loading (as indeed it will be).

More impactful than clubs, which tend to be brief in duration and sparsely attended despite teachers' best efforts, are whole-school "drop down days": time when every pupil in the school takes part in something which takes them beyond the curriculum. In this way, you ensure that every pupil benefits from the enriching experiences on offer. When these experiences are well chosen, I become a real advocate of this non-academic curriculum because suddenly every pupil benefits and the experiences are beneficial to their knowledge and wider lives beyond school.

Even so, in the many schools I've worked at which do this, attendance tended to dip on these days. Leaders need to communicate and over-communicate with pupils and parents the importance of such events. Have a representative pupil committee to feed into the planning of them, or put aside a form time or part of a PSHE lesson for pupils to say what they think would be enriching (and narrate why enriching experiences are important, so they don't all say "go to Thorpe Park") to secure buy-in.

Think widely about the experiences you want your pupils to have that they might not get through their day-to-day lives. Many pupils (though certainly not all) will visit a theme park; most will not attend a museum or art gallery of their own organisation and choosing. I've worked in schools that manage to get a whole year group over to France for the day, albeit with many pupils paying a voluntary contribution, and this can be really formative, even life-changing, for children.

At the same time, you must carefully balance the time and energy it takes teachers to plan and execute trips with their workload for delivering on the basic curriculum effectively. Where your curriculum needs work, stripping back on extra-curricular demands seems like a sensible choice. Any trips you can run annually with minimal additional workload should be considered; any departments where the curriculum and attainment are strong or teachers are underloaded should be leaned on to carry the extra-curricular offer, and this should be carefully narrated in a way that makes them feel they are valued and they are doing something important in the time they might have earmarked to go home early, for example.

## Careers education

In the UK, secondary schools are bound by the Gatsby benchmarks, which are that schools need to run a stable careers programme, learn from career and labour market information, address the needs of each pupil, link curriculum learning to careers, establish and ensure that encounters with employers and employees happen, ensure that pupils experience the workplace as well as have encounters with further and higher education and benefit from personal guidance.

For some schools, this is well embedded and feels "standard." For other schools, this is a broad and demanding list that feels challenging. My experience is that the Gatsby demands of a careers education are often challenging to meet in a busy, understaffed, and underfunded school, and it is from that perspective I write.

Firstly, as should be obvious from the enormous and demanding list above, someone senior needs to have named responsibility for careers education. That doesn't mean they need to do all the work, but they do need to hold the responsibility for its being done and done well. Secondly, leaders need to give an individual time and resource to ensure that the work can be done. The work is time-consuming and at times administrative and ought to be recognised by a decent-sized teaching and learning responsibility (TLR) as well, ideally, as a decent amount of time. Given the breadth and scope, it might make sense to make your careers lead a sort of HoD, much like the broad spanning Head of PSHE role suggested previously. They will benefit from the same kind of curriculum planning and thinking that your subject HoDs will.

Secondly, ensure that you lead this individual with real clarity. Leaders need to have a clear sense of what they want and expect of the role, or the individual will not be able to gain traction in their work. The role of a middle leader is a tough one, but for middle leaders who must orchestrate teachers to do work outside their subject, it is a difficult ask – don't make their job harder.

Thirdly, ensure that there is sufficient budget and curriculum time to ensure that your vision for careers can be meaningfully achieved. Providing wider experiences and work experience does not come without additional cost, so be prepared to spend for a successful and fulfilling offer.

## What do secondary teachers need to know about the primary curriculum?

As someone who went from a fully secondary teaching background to running a large all-through 3-18 pupil school, I had to learn a lot about the primary curriculum in a very short space of time in order to lead effectively, and this is work I've continued to do in my role at the National Institute of Teaching in designing programmes that work for participants across the phases.

The first, and probably blindingly obvious, fact to state is that almost every primary school assigns one teacher to one class. That teacher is responsible for teaching almost all, and sometimes all, of the curriculum. They need, therefore, to be able to deliver great lessons in as diverse a realm as Maths, English, Humanities, arts and creative subjects, PE, and languages. It is a feat that secondary teachers would baulk at. If we are asking secondary subject experts to understand the full sweep of the curriculum – what came before and what will come next so we can situate each year group carefully within this – the order is far taller for primary teachers.

The curriculum will also look dramatically different in reception and Early Years to Key Stages 1 and then 2. The role of play in developing children's learning has been outlined earlier in this chapter, so we won't cover that ground again.

The other aspect that causes much controversy for secondary teachers is the degree to which writing is scaffolded in primary. I'd often be surprised to pick up a beautiful page and a half of prose from a year 6 student only to discover it had been written over the course of an entire week, and every child's book was practically the same, word for word, piece of writing.

Inevitably, primary leaders will want to prioritise core subjects, particularly Maths, Reading, and Writing as these are ultimately the subjects the pupils take nationally standardised tests in. Remembering Hirsch's edict from earlier still stands – indeed, Hirsch writes primarily about primary education. The broader the humanities and science reading children do, the better their reading, writing, and understanding will ultimately be.

## What do primary teachers need to know about the secondary curriculum?

Similarly, colleagues leading in the primary phase must have an eye to what they are preparing their pupils for. From the feedback I've heard from primary colleagues on secondary lessons, their chief concern is that year 7 lessons are pitched too low and revisit prior learning, duplicating what children already know securely. By the same token, secondary colleagues are often concerned that their year 7s find material overly challenging.

Primary leaders should be aware that it is a challenge to pitch year 7 adequately to meet the curriculum and learning needs of children who often come from ten or more different primary feeder schools. What will be basic and duplication for some children will be unfamiliar and out of reach for others. Where content is duplicated, often scaffolds are minimised or removed, and so children who may well be familiar with material appear to struggle when working largely independently, a feature of much secondary lesson work. In the absence of a more didactic national curriculum in primary, this is bound to happen, and secondary teachers know the struggle of teaching children with the full range of prior knowledge.

The other challenge in secondary school is the number and variety of new teachers pupils will encounter and work with. We know that pupil attainment "dips" at moments of transition, and part of this is due to the change in routines and teachers: where pupil working memory is taken up thinking about new routines and new people, they are less able to focus fully on their learning and so learn less. We see this in secondary schools where pupils move from one teacher to another – I've seen children with incredibly strong knowledge seem to forget it all in the first week with a new teacher, even when the teacher uses consciously chosen similar words to describe previously studied units.

Pupils at secondary school benefit from being taught by subject experts, and this can be a particular strength where their primaries might have been less strong. One area of challenge is languages, where children rarely arrive at secondary school with the same prior knowledge; indeed, they have rarely all studied the same language. Primary teachers should therefore focus on fundamentals and transferable aspects of language learning, such as common etymology and common grammatical approaches, to ensure that pupils gain something from their primary language teaching, even though they may not go on to study that language at secondary school.

Most secondary teachers I know would rather pupils arrived in year 7 with a strong grasp of reading, writing, and numeracy; some teachers complain of unpicking misconceptions that have perhaps been inevitably embedded by non-subject experts. This means that a robust, rigorously written primary curriculum is key, and involving subject experts in the creation of this is an essential way to safeguard pupils' future learning. Put simply, if you aren't sure, best to say nothing and check it later: it is far harder to un-learn knowledge.

## Key takeaways

- Teachers can't teach great lessons if they aren't teaching a rich, worthwhile, well-sequenced curriculum.

- Support middle leaders to fully grasp, own, and inhabit their curriculum – even if it isn't the exact one they would have ideally chosen themselves.

- The curriculum is never "finished": build time and support leaders to invest repeated time in refining it.

- Care more about getting formative assessment right.

- Treat the non-academic curriculum with the seriousness you treat the academic curriculum.

With the curriculum prioritised and embedded, we are ready to move on to our penultimate chapter: teaching. This is where we support colleagues to ensure that the curriculum is well delivered, so children are able to learn and remember it.

## Notes

1 E.D. Hirsch *Why Knowledge Matters* Harvard Education Press 2016 p. 171.
2 E.D. Hirsch *Cultural Literacy* Vintage, 1988.
3 John Hattie *Visible Learning: The Sequel* Routledge, 2023 pp. 186–7.
4 "As soon as students get a grade, the learning stops." Dylan Wiliam *Embedded Formative Assessment* Solution Tree Press 2011 p. 123.
5 "Without a strong foundation of knowledge, the application of reading comprehension strategies is limited." https://educationendowmentfoundation.org.uk/news/eef-blog-the-dna-of-reading-comprehension-knowledge-skills-and-strategies accessed 23.9.23.
6 Barak Rosenshine "Principles of Instruction" American Educator 2012 https://www.aft.org/sites/default/files/Rosenshine.pdf.
7 EEF: Special educational needs in mainstream schools, 2020 https://d2tic4wvo1iusb.cloudfront.net/production/eef-guidance-reports/send/EEF_Special_Educational_Needs_in_Mainstream_Schools_Guidance_Report.pdf?v=1695537818 Accessed 24.9.23.
8 The campaign group Parents and Teachers for Excellence collated a list from December 2018 to July 2019 and found 114 suggestions in mainstream media, ranging from meditation to cold water shock: https://parentsandteachers.org.uk/resources/what-should-schools-teach/.
9 According to government figures for 2022.

# 3 Leading teaching

Once school leaders have established whole-school behaviour routines and a rigorous, academic curriculum that meets the needs of all pupils, the next aspect to prioritise is teaching. There is a wealth of evidence to suggest that the quality of the teacher is the single greatest aspect within our control to improve pupil outcomes.[1] Not only does the quality of teaching have a dramatic impact on pupils, it is not a static aspect: teachers, all of them, can improve.

This is a particularly important point in a teacher recruitment crisis, but it will never actually stop being important: however good any teacher is, they can always get better. Dylan Wiliam puts this perfectly: "Every teacher needs to improve, not because they are not good enough, but because they can be even better."[2] There will always be a better way of doing everything on this earth, and we evolve as the years go on, so no teacher is the "finished product."

That makes teacher professional development crucial to get right when leading a school, and so that is where we will begin. We'll go on to think more about the systems and structures that leaders use to help teachers improve, such as coaching, the role of middle leaders in improving teaching, how to monitor and evaluate teaching practice, and how leaders might adapt teaching for particular groups of pupils.

## Professional development

In my earlier books, I describe whole-school continuing professional development (CPD) as the ultimate mixed-ability class: you have brand-new trainee teachers sitting next to colleagues who have been teaching ten or twenty years; you have Maths teachers working alongside physical education (PE) teachers. This is a good thing in some ways: of course, you want everyone to have a shared approach to teaching, because, as emphasised in Chapter 1 on behaviour, when colleagues all follow a shared approach to lesson routines, everyone benefits.

That said, it is a tall ask to develop teachers from such varied starting points and backgrounds in the same room. It is no wonder that so many teachers resent the hour spent in the hall listening to a leader speak, wishing they'd brought their marking along, or surreptitiously answering emails on a partially concealed device. Has any whole-school CPD ever changed a teacher's practice? Probably, but I couldn't personally point to a session that I'd say changed mine.

This is perhaps because not enough professional development prioritises getting teachers to actually practice what they do in the classroom. Doug Lemov's training sessions are renowned the world over for having impact on teachers' practice, and I suspect a large part of this (alongside the well-deserved renown from the world-class expertise of the facilitators) is that the sessions make teachers get up and actually try out doing things a bit differently. It is this action that makes it more likely to impact their practice in a real classroom full of children.

Changing what we do in the classroom is a challenge: Peps McCrea notes that "in the classroom, we face a vast sea of information to process and decisions to make. To simply *survive* this situation, it is necessary to automate large swathes of teaching."[3] This is great for efficient, stress-free teaching but very bad when we try to get teachers to change what they are doing. The reason teachers don't do what they've learned how to do in CPD sessions is probably not through stubborn refusal but simply through force of habit: if they've handed out books one way for the past eight years, it is no small ask to get them to do it in a different way, for example.

Adding live practice to CPD is an essential first step to getting new habits embedded and used in the day-to-day classroom. If you've had teachers sitting passively in CPD sessions, this will be a challenge to narrate. Leaders will need to model going "all in" with practice, embracing the sense of awkwardness that inevitably comes from performing in front of peers. Leaders also need to facilitate this well: using small groups with high-trust relationships, such as department teams, will help to make this process less painful. Once this is normalised, you can start to shake up the groups and have teachers work with others, or you can pair them to have experienced teachers guiding newbies, for example.

In my experience, schools fall into one of two camps: either too much time spent on professional development or not enough. I can hear the quizzical question from the keen readers of this book: "too much?"

Yes – I've worked in schools with an hour or more protected time for CPD each week. This is an enormous amount of time, particularly if we're talking about something whole-staff and led in the main hall, for example. The challenge of this is: what is being presented? What are you doing for an hour to make the most of staff time?

Too often, that hour is taken up by a meaty aspect of pedagogy and followed up the next week with another meaty aspect of pedagogy. We are given time, and we want to make the most of it, but in spreading our focus too wide, we run the risk of doing nothing well. It takes time to embed practice.

Conversely, at one school I worked at, we spent half an hour once or twice a half term on professional development. It felt like a decent-length session but quite challenging to practice the technique with staff and hard to check in and find out how it was going in the interim.

I'd suggest a model that is halfway between these two. I'd have a weekly, but very short, touch point. Perhaps the initial session could be longer, but the following weeks would best be spent reflecting on the same practice (How did it go? Did you use the technique/idea? What were the challenges?) and practising it over and over again with colleagues. By doing something over a longer period of time, we are more likely to be able to fold it into our regular practice.

There is, of course, no hard and fast rule. I know of one successful trust that reserves 30 minutes a *day* for teachers to practise their craft together in small groups, and by all accounts, teaching and learning and teacher development are second to none there. What matters, perhaps, is not the time and its allocation but how it is planned and used.

Therefore, it is important to take regular feedback on your professional development offer as well as to check with a critical eye on impact. Find out from teachers, anonymously, how they found the session: was it helpful, did they change what they were doing as a result, would they suggest any improvements or next steps? Make teachers do this *during* the session – if you send out a survey after working hours, be ready to hear only from your most engaged and happy team members. Next, equally important, do joint learning walks as senior leaders to check on impact: is the stuff of CPD being practised in classrooms? How widespread and effective is it? Can leaders move on to the next thing, or does this need further input to be secured?

Above all, resist the urge to move on before something is secure. Even if this means cancelling CPD for most staff and just working with a small group who need more time, best to get everyone meeting a minimum bar before sweeping onto the next thing just because that's what your year plan says to do.

---

**Lindsay Galbraith, an Assistant Vice Principal for teaching and learning, shares how her approach to designing professional development has evolved**

*Every year, staff complete a survey to evaluate our professional development programme. And every year until recently, staff would ask for more autonomy to be able to pursue their own interests and their own specific areas for development. The internal crisis I had was this: we were expecting Ofsted (Office for Standards in Education, Children's Services and Skills), there were clearly whole-school needs that professional development needed to help to improve, but how do I ensure that staff also are given autonomy to develop themselves?*

*I felt like I was walking on a high wire, balancing the needs of the school with the needs of individuals. Whilst other schools were launching coaching programmes to give a more personalised development system, we did not have the capacity to do this in the short term.*

*My first step to tackle this issue was to redefine what the purpose of professional development was in my setting. I worked with the other senior and middle leaders to gain further insight into the value and vision for professional development. We had to be mindful of where we were at as a school and a staff body. We had to prioritise what the school needed, and I was very honest with middle leaders about these needs. As leaders, we must make decisions that are going to have the biggest impact on the children that we teach.*

*Once we had determined this, I worked alongside Curriculum Leaders to divide our time up. Our whole-school CPD would focus on the vision and priorities of the school. Our old-style department meetings would now be focused on subject development and time given to individual and departmental priorities.*

*With priorities and vision agreed and aligned, the design for professional development became the next priority. Previously, I mapped the whole year, with a core focus and set aims and objectives of each session. This did not work! Schools are a changeable beast; you can plan excellent session focusses but things change; priorities change.*

*This was highlighted for me during a Trust Walk Around. Alongside the Executive Principal of the Trust, we walked around the building focusing on the starts of lessons. We both identified that whilst retrieval was embedded into teacher practice, checking for understanding before moving on was not. Our whole-school CPD session was that evening and I had already planned the session, but this became the priority. Thus, I scrapped the original plan and used the walk around as the basis to discuss checking for understanding. No PowerPoint, no resources, just what I had seen and what we needed to do about it. Still to this day, staff will always remember this session as the most impactful session because I could draw upon the day's events and be very specific about the need to improve.*

*Therefore, I now design the core focused theme for the year and alongside this react much more to the needs of our school through culture walks and leaders' identified development areas.*

## Abby Hughes, Assistant Headteacher for Teaching and Learning at the West London Free School, explores how to launch a new teaching and learning strategy with all staff

*Introducing any kind of new initiative and getting it to stick is difficult, especially in a well-established school. To generate any meaningful buy-in from pupils and staff, there must be a clear "why" behind it. What is the existing problem and how is this new initiative going to address it? We've recently introduced whole-school use of mini-whiteboards (MWBs) in lessons. Cold-call was already well embedded, but we were becoming increasingly conscious that it couldn't maximise the number of pupils thinking in the way that MWBs can.*

*There were a number of steps I took when launching to staff and pupils that I think are applicable to the introduction of any new system in a school:*

1 *Become an expert: visit other schools, talk to their staff, watch and read and think about the different options and potential pitfalls. This is instrumental when it comes to planning. Find out the ways it can be go wrong so that these can be pre-empted in staff training and observers can be vigilant for them.*

2 *Get down to the nitty gritty: how will this new initiative actually work in a way that prevents any lost learning time? At West London Free School, teachers don't have their own classroom, so MWB distribution was a sticking point. We decided that we would give pupils their own MWB equipment to carry around with them. This meant no lost learning time handing them out and in, and no worrying about who has taken the box of MWBs from a classroom. We also thought about the simplest way of labelling equipment, how to prevent pupils from getting multiple equipment sanctions across the day, and what pupils do if they lose equipment. The nitty gritty is where initiatives can come unstuck so it's important to think hard about the logistics.*

3 *Create a shared language/routine/system: If pupils know that they're doing exactly the same thing with exactly the same cues in every lesson, a new initiative will become automatised far more quickly. Think carefully about the precise routine, and how it will mitigate against the pitfalls you've identified. We knew that MWB use becomes redundant if pupils are looking at each other's MWB for the answer. As such, holding the board close to you and hovering it over the desk (which I'd seen at another school I'd visited) became part of our shared routine.*

4 *Try it yourself: A trial run is an amazing way of discovering the issues that you haven't thought of in the planning process so far. I tried the new MWB routine I'd devised with three different classes and filmed myself each time. Between each delivery, I watched the video and tweaked the routine. By the end of this process, the routine was much slicker and I felt ready to introduce it to staff.*

5 *Model it to staff: After doing the big sell to all staff, we split into smaller groups. A colleague and I, who had watched the video of me doing the routine, modelled the form-time where MWBs were being launched to pupils. Asking staff to act as pupils felt silly at first, but the sessions actually felt really upbeat. Crucially, it allowed staff to see for themselves the language and routine they needed to follow. The session followed a script I had created, which was then distributed to staff afterwards.*

6 *Watch it in action: Watch the new system in action as much as you can in the days after its launch. I was looking for universality, lethal mutations, and any stumbling blocks. I then considered whether these were just teething problems, whether more training was needed for some staff, or whether the system needed to be altered wholesale. I sought to enact these changes as swiftly as possible: once a deviation has become embedded, it becomes more difficult to rectify.*

7 *Don't let the honeymoon period fool you: After any launch, there is inevitably a time of fervent uptake. This does peter out. Guard against this by planning in training sessions which highlight the new initiative at key points through the year. Talk about it in briefings and when you give feedback to staff. If its importance is not continually narrated from the top, it can quickly disappear.*

---

**Maria Craster, Assistant Principal at One Degree Academy in London, shares her approach to refining teacher professional development in a growing school and ensuring consistency and impact**

*At One Degree Academy, we believe that all students deserve the best teacher in front of them. We looked at research as to how to best ensure this and made some strategic choices: embed a shared language and consistent teaching approach across the school, build a culture of feedback, and getting better through incremental changes. The cultural aspect of this is paramount but, for the purpose of this example, we are going to fast forward to when we had a larger school with an established culture of improvement.*

When I took over as lead on staff development most teachers were used to regular feedback, coaching and taking part in training which involved rehearsal, however these sessions weren't codified. I felt they could be made more consistent. We also had gone from a very small team where we were able to follow a model of everyone, including teaching assistants, getting coached every week for half an hour, to a considerably larger team where this was no longer possible. Scaling up the staff development model and ensuring it remained of a high standard were two significant challenges.

Firstly, we looked at how to scale the model. I decided to put this on hold temporarily and instead focus on the consistency of coaching by the leaders in the school. We signed up to The Coaching Collective and ran fortnightly training sessions as a group, checking in as a team on our coaching and bringing challenges from our sessions to sense-check our highest leverage next steps. I wanted to ensure that all staff received the best offer regardless of their coach. I asked coaches to share the times that they were coaching with me so that I was able to check in and give feedback on their coaching. Using a centralised online platform helped me to be able to do this more efficiently.

Gradually, we increased the number of coaches, first supporting teachers (not Initial Teacher Training [ITT] or Early Career Teaching [ECT]) to give drop-ins with quick wins to their teaching assistants (It was effective when … / Next time try) and then building them up to coaching other teachers in the team. I decided to keep my expert coaches working with our novice teachers, as they had the most to learn, as well as peer coaching our other expert teachers, as generally their coaching required more experienced hands to spot their next action step. This model is ongoing and the team is still growing as our school does.

In terms of our whole-school training sessions, previously a different member of Senior Leadership Team (SLT) had led our "Deliberate Practice" training sessions each week. However, I decided that these sessions would be more consistent if I had sole responsibility for their delivery. I looked at the Education Endowment Foundation's (EEF's) paper on Effective Professional Development and decided to focus on the mechanisms that it mentions. This meant I was able to create a clear template for sessions including: reflection, target setting, reading of quality literature, watching high quality examples (of our school and others), rehearsal, feedback and providing a clear success criteria prompt.

I created a skeleton plan of each week's 30-minute session, using Doug Lemov's Teach Like a Champion[4] as a starting point with general themes for each half term (for example, Autumn Term: Managing Behaviour). In our weekly SLT Meetings, we look at what the training is supposed to be the following week and then check if that fits in as the highest leverage training based on our informal learning walks that week. I find this flexible model of planning content for training has helped ensure a good coverage of techniques whilst still adapting to the needs of the staff.

## Instructional coaching

An aspect of professional development that has gained much traction in recent years is instructional coaching. As far as I know, this was first mooted in Paul Bambrick-Santoyo's hugely influential *Leverage Leadership*. In this book, Bambrick-Santoyo outlines how leaders might quality-assure lessons by visiting them, staying a short amount of time, and identifying what is going really well and what needs to improve further. In outlining the approach to teacher observation, he writes:

> teacher feedback is not about the volume of observations or the length of written feedback; it's about bite-sized action steps that allow a teacher to grow systematically from novice to proficient to master teacher... You don't get [great] results by placing your best teachers strategically – you get them by coaching each and every teacher to do excellent work.[5]

The chief benefit of instructional coaching is that it is immediate and bespoke feedback to individual teachers. The argument goes: if we want to improve what teachers are doing, small-step feedback delivered soon after live practice is a sure-fire way to go. The evidence would seem to agree.[6] It also has the benefits of circumventing the issues of whole-staff CPD outlined in the previous section and being extremely personalised to teachers.

There are some who argue that this feedback needs to be delivered by subject experts, and at a certain point, there is some truth in this. While non-subject experts can give coaching feedback on routines and general teaching practices, they won't be able to spot and advise on the nuances of explanations and preventing misconceptions. It is also a challenge to advise on practical subjects when you teach a traditional subject, and vice versa: your classrooms will and should look a bit different to get the best out of pupils. Nonetheless, for leaders looking to incrementally improve the practice of teachers, employing instructional coaching is a good bet.

One challenge of coaching is the availability of individuals who have the experience and expertise to do it. I heard of a horror story where a colleague trained leaders in how to give coaching feedback but later learned they didn't know what great teaching practice looked like and so had inadvertently become experts in embedding really bad practice. First, start with individuals who are aligned in what great teaching means – they need to be great practitioners themselves, or others are less likely to take their feedback on board, and they need to know how to communicate what needs to come next. If you go into a chaotic room, your action step probably won't be around quality of questioning, for example.

The next challenge is the time coaching takes, and the good news is that it need not take long. I worked in one school that really went for it with coaching, and every member of staff had a 20-minute observation followed by a 40-minute coaching session. The school set the bar so high that when crunch time came and people were covering lessons, the time simply slipped away and they weren't able to complete coaching.

The best coaching I've experienced as a practitioner was extremely time-light. I had a weekly observation of only five to ten minutes, which started out as a daily observation for my first two weeks in post. Instead of having a meeting with feedback, I'd get a short email after these lesson visits. At first, the email would have four or five positive bullet points before a one-line "next step": the thing I could tweak to be better next time. Over time, that shrank to just feedback on my progress on the last action step and another one-line next step, because my coach had built the relationship and trust so I simply wanted the feedback – I didn't need to be told what was going well anymore, just reassured I was actioning the feedback. Because the observations were incredibly frequent, they could be incredibly short – this person knew my practice and could spot what was a one-off mistake I didn't normally make as opposed to regular quirks of my practice we wanted to iron out.

Brief but happening is always preferable to in-depth but not happening. This is especially important for schools with limited capacity for coaching.

The final hurdle I've experienced with instructional coaching is teachers who don't want to be observed. Indeed, in some schools, there is no open-door policy or culture of lesson drop-ins, which makes instructional coaching incredibly tough to get off the ground.

I experienced this as a Head of Department, and so instead I did a couple of things. First, I worked only with teachers who wanted to be coached. I laid out what instructional coaching was, presented it as a trial or experiment we'd all explore together, and asked if anyone was interested. Only two people were, but they were so positive and enthusiastic about the premise it built a really positive feeling about it.

Even if your team aren't keen and your school aren't up for supporting you to implement coaching, you can still use a coaching approach to aspects like learning walks which are normally ubiquitous in self-evaluation of departments. Ensuring that you're giving developmental feedback following any observation, no matter how short, which people find useful and which is delivered in an unthreatening way is a good way in to getting individuals to value coaching.

For a short time, I worked only a couple of days a week in a school to support improving their teaching, and here it was especially important to build relationships fast so people didn't feel threatened when I came into their rooms. Luckily, the school had established an open-door policy, so it wasn't unusual to have someone in lessons. With this school, I made sure the first week of observations I sent only positive feedback – and lots of it. I searched for every good thing colleagues were doing, and I told them. I'm a firm believer that it is also developmental to tell people what they do well, as so often teachers have no idea what they're doing that is working, and if they don't know that, it could disappear as they try to do something different or additional in the future.

The second week of lesson visits, I stuck with at least three positive bullet points and went with one small action step I felt could move their teaching on. In all my time with the school, I stuck to this ratio of at least three to one, praise to development, because I wasn't going to be present in the school long enough (one single year, two days a week) to build relationships to do anything less or more than that.

Clearly, there are far more thorough ways of implementing instructional coaching, and you'll read an example of this next. I hope what I've shared is that you don't need to let the best be the enemy of the good: you can do coaching to some degree no matter what your capacity and team buy-in.

---

### Dave Tushingham, Lead Practitioner Maths, Greenshaw Learning Trust, explains how low-stakes developmental drop-ins work in his school

*We all fundamentally learn in the same way. Although adults have significantly more and more varied experiences to draw from than children, the science of learning remains constant. As teachers, we implement classroom strategies with our students, measure the impact through a reflective process and refine what we do. Having a clear set of teaching principles to work from based on the science of learning helps us to frame our practice and our reflections. I believe the same holds true when we coach adults.*

*The Greenshaw Learning Trust use a low-stakes developmental drop-in (DDI) process to support teachers' classroom development:*

- *Drop-ins happen every two weeks*

- *They last approximately ten minutes*

- *They are low-stakes – they don't contribute to performance management in any way*

- *Feedback is given within 48 hours*

- *Three to five strengths are shared in the feedback*

- *A highest leverage actionable step is agreed between the visitor and the teacher.[7]*

*The feedback is given based on a set of core teaching principles, and the action step is revisited in the next cycle of drop-ins. If the action step is not relevant within the next drop-in, the teacher visited will have an opportunity to share their progress for their action step when receiving their feedback.*

*A similar model can be applied to the delivery of staff CPD. To be impactful, it is important to think about what's the same and what's different between teaching students and coaching staff so that the model can be adapted to maximise impact. Here are a few examples:*

*Teaching Students versus Coaching Staff*

| What's the same? | What's different? |
| --- | --- |
| The Science of Learning | Adult learners have reduced cognitive capacity through other responsibilities. |
| There is identified knowledge that requires teaching. | Adult learners are more expert in how to learn independently. |
| There will be emotional barriers to learning (stress, personal events). | The type of relationships and interpersonal dynamics |
| There will be active learners and more reluctant learners. | Reasons for attending the learning episode differs (pay versus legal requirement) |
| Learning episodes are timetabled. | The frequency of the learning episode |

## Josh Goodrich, founder and CEO of Steplab, Former Trust Professional Development Lead, and author of Responsive Coaching (2024), shares the key challenges and some potential solutions to running instructional coaching successfully in schools

*Great teachers make a huge difference to students' lives. Helping teachers to improve throughout their career is vital. But how can we best do this?*

*Multiple studies suggest that Instructional Coaching (IC)—a school-centred approach to developing teachers—is one of the best bets we have. But many key texts define IC differently. This can often go beyond surface features and right to the heart of what it is that coaches should be doing when they work with teachers. IC promises to generate results for teachers above and beyond other forms of professional development (PD), yet we can't design an effective coaching programme unless we are clear on what it is and who it's for.*

*To overcome this problem, it's important to look beyond labels. Whether we are doing "Directive" or "Facilitative" IC is far less important than which mechanisms our coaching contains. In a wide-ranging, comprehensive meta-study, Sam Sims and colleagues have found that PD that incorporates elements from each of four key "categories" – building insights, setting clear goals, sharing precise techniques and doing rehearsal – has a substantial impact on teacher quality and student attainment.[8] Coaches are in a unique position to work with teachers to develop contextual insights around teaching, help teachers work towards worthwhile classroom goals, model the right techniques to use to achieve these, and ensure that these are implemented skilfully using rehearsal.*

*But, importantly, if any of these mechanisms - particularly modelling and rehearsal – are absent from coaching, it's unlikely to have the desired effect.*

*Based on conversations with school leaders, experience implementing coaching across schools and multi-academy trusts (MATs), and key research, we can identify four key persistent challenges that drive successful implementation:*

1 **Professional Culture**: How can we develop a culture of openness to feedback and commitment to ongoing development?

2 **Training**: How we can recruit and train a team of skilled, knowledgeable coaches?

3 **Systems design**: How should we structure our programme so that it delivers results in a way that balances with other school systems, and delivers efficiency?

4 **Responsive Leadership**: How can we gather information about what's happening when our programme is up and running? How can we respond effectively to address issues and deliver continued improvement?

## Professional Culture

1 Are teachers at your school open to regular visits to lessons?

2 Do teachers welcome feedback without feeling that they are being judged?

3 Do teachers actively seek out opportunities to collaborate to improve their practice?

- **IC not Performance Management**: Ensure a full split of IC from judgemental performance management. Aim to get rid of "graded" lesson visits.

- **Equalise it**: Build a sense of IC as an egalitarian practice by recruiting widely for your initial team of coaches: move beyond SLT and look into using middle and pastoral leaders and beyond.

- **Open-door drop-ins**: Build an open-door culture by encouraging staff to give regular, short, "zero-stakes" drop-ins. If necessary, begin with positive feedback only, before moving to developmental over time.

- **Make it optional**: Begin by having coaching as an optional practice. Allow a "buzz" about coaching to grow so that staff feel safe.

- **Use "whole group" coaching**: Ensure that staff are familiar and comfortable with some of the key mechanisms of IC, like modelling and rehearsal, by including these as key components of your whole-staff PD before moving to full coaching.

## Training

1 Do teachers have clear mental models for what good teaching should look like at your school? Is there a shared language in place for how teachers talk about practice?

2 Do you have a team of willing volunteers to become coaches, recruited from all areas of the school (rather than just from SLT)?

3 Do you offer coaches regular training and feedback to sharpen their skills?

   - **Set the standard**: Develop a clear vision of what great teaching looks like in your context, including standardised language and video of great teachers modelling in action.

   - **Start slowly and snowball**: Don't rush into coaching for all. If necessary, recruit a small team, train them, and have them coach each other. Once they're ready, unleash them on an initial group of teachers. Then flip those teachers up as coaches and repeat.

   - **Create competence**: Once you've recruited your initial coaching team, spend time training them in your vision of great teaching as well as in key areas of coaching expert knowledge and skill, like how to model and lead rehearsal.

   - **Coach-on-coaching**: Keep an eye on the strengths and weaknesses of your team as they develop by conducting regular "coaching-on-coaching." Visit lessons with your coaches, discuss these with them, watch their feedback meetings, and then coach them to improve their skills.

## Systems design

1 Do coaches and teachers have the time and space to prioritise coaching observations and feedback rather than having to use their frees or find time in the day?

2 Have other PD and meetings structures been removed or pared back to make room for coaching to succeed?

3 Does coaching feel like a critical, vital priority to all staff?

   - **Consider costs**: Carefully consider the costs of IC for coaches and teachers: for coaches, each new coachee adds around 15 minutes for the lesson observation and 30 minutes for the feedback meeting.

   - **Work the ratios**: Manage this by working on your coach-to-teacher ratio, ideally 1:1. Higher ratios may be manageable for senior leaders or those with dedicated time assigned to coach but may prove too much for others. If your ratio of teachers to coaches is too high, you may need to recruit and train more coaches.

- **Provide time**: Give coaches time they need for observing lessons by removing other priorities. Ensure that the free periods are "guaranteed" lesson observation time by committing to avoid loading them with duties and similar.

- **Re-purpose meetings**: Solve the "time for coaching" issue in one go by providing dedicated time for coaches and teachers to complete feedback. One method that has worked well in many UK schools is to re-purpose a weekly staff meeting.

- **Message importance**: We wouldn't ever miss a lesson in school, so why would we skip our all-important observation and feedback time?

## Responsive Leadership

1 Do you gather data on completion (is it happening?) and quality (is it good?) of the coaching in your school?

2 Do you take action to improve completion of coaching by holding coaches accountable? Do you take action to improve quality through giving coaches feedback?

3 Do you regularly meet with leaders to discuss and implement improvements to your programme (e.g. recruiting more coaches or upgrading your vision of excellent teaching)?

- **Improve completion**: Gather and analyse data around completion of coaching observations & feedback meetings. Intervene early when coaching isn't taking place so that your coaches build lasting habits.

- **Recognise effort**: Build a culture where coaches feel valued for their hard work by taking the time to recognise coaches that are getting the job done well, week-in, week-out.

- **Improve quality**: Gather and analyse data about the quality of coaching feedback. Intervene early to address potential weaker-quality coaching through providing additional training and using coaching-on-coaching.

- **Compare with reality**: Cross-reference your data against the reality of teachers' classrooms. Ask your Teaching and Learning (T&L) and SLT teams to take a history of teacher action steps on a learning walk: are teachers really using these in their classrooms? Do they appear to be improving learning?

## Inducting new staff

A school can change dramatically between one year and the next, as few schools experience zero teacher turnover, and a school – perhaps more than any other organisation – is made up of its teachers and the relationships they build between pupils and one another.

Clearly, how we work with those new to our teams is imperative. I've written about how we might induct new teachers in *Culture Rules*, and essentially it boils down to the following:

- Ensure that new leaders visit the school as many times as they are freed up to, including after-school drop-ins.

- Let them know the concrete specifics as well as the softer stuff – what their team is like and what is working or not working in managing it.

- Organise one day for all new staff to come in, ensuring that they can meet one another as well as making it less of a time drain for existing staff to run sessions.

- Consider induction sessions around mission, staff culture, school priorities, curriculum, pupil ethos, and teaching approach.

- When the school year begins, build in extra drop-ins for new teachers to continually check in on how they are doing and any questions they may have.

---

**Abby Hughes, Assistant Headteacher for Teaching and Learning at the West London Free School, details how new teachers are inducted at West London Free School**

*Joining a new school can be tough. Our new staff induction programme has two aims. Firstly, we want to remove any obstacles that may prevent new staff from having a smooth start. Secondly, we want to induct new staff into our "house-style" of teaching so that we have consistency between lessons and so they feel like successful West London Free School teachers as quickly as possible.*

*At the start of the school year, we have a New Staff Induction afternoon ahead of whole-staff inset.*

*The schedule we follow is below:*

| | |
|---|---|
| Lunch with the SLT and Heads of Department (HoDs) | An opportunity to ensure that all new staff are known by the SLT and vice versa. It also gives our Headteacher the opportunity to accrue some facts about each new member of staff that he uses when introducing them to whole-staff the next day. |
| Welcome address from the Headteacher | An overview of the ethos of the school and what we are working towards. |
| School tour | This focusses on the granular things that are unlikely to have been covered at interview (e.g. where the toilets are, how the coffee machines and the printers work, staffroom etiquette). |
| Collection of important documents and school equipment | Staff Handbook, timetable, duty list, classroom keys, staff pass, laptop, log-in details etc. are all distributed. We have our information technology (IT) team on hand to troubleshoot any IT issues immediately. |
| Behaviour and Rewards at West London Free School | A brief run-down of what staff need to know for the delivery of their first lessons e.g. what we call each consequence, what they are given for, and how to issue them. |
| Teaching and learning at West London Free School | In a similar vein, this is a need-to-know run-down of our whole-school teaching and learning routines that staff should use from the outset (e.g. our means of getting pupil attention and entrance and exit routines). |
| Introduction to the personal development curriculum | Many new staff are form tutors so have to deliver our personal development curriculum. In these sessions, staff are teaching out of specialism, so we provide some initial training on how to plan these sessions and how to deal with the sensitive nature of some of these topics. |

*Following this initial induction day, our new staff induction programme continues on Friday mornings across the next seven weeks. It is during this period that we induct new staff into what it means to be a West London Free School teacher.*

*Each Friday morning, new staff have a session on one of our 7 Principles of a lesson. These focus on the two or three teaching strategies that we believe to be the most impactful in achieving that principle. These sessions are supported by our "7 Principles Core Reader," our teaching and learning handbook that all new staff are sent before joining. It contains an explanation of each of these strategies and links to further reading on them.*

*Each new staff member is assigned a coach for this period. In the week following the training session, this coach will drop-in to observe the new staff member at least twice and particularly look for the strategies that had been covered in the session. They then record precise praise and granular improvement targets in a New Staff Induction record. New staff also have to conduct at least one observation of another staff member each week, recording their reflections in their New Staff Induction record. The new staff member and coach have a weekly meeting slot where they meet to discuss the feedback further and cover anything else that the new staff member needs support with.*

*It is our hope that by the end of that first half-term, new staff have received enough support that has enabled them to be able to quickly embrace and embed the West London Free School way. It also allows more experienced staff to quickly spot any challenges the new staff member may be facing and nip them in the bud.*

## Supporting middle leaders: developing department teams

Often a key individual you, as a senior leader, will "work through" is a middle leader. While Heads of Year have enormous influence over pupils, they rarely directly line-manage individuals, and so the usual route for senior leaders to improve teaching in schools is through department leads.

You will want to make talk about their team a key focus of your touch-point meetings. With departments, it is easy to get drawn into administrative talk, particularly around compliance aspects such as exams, and this is, of course, important – as is curriculum development. But you also need to ensure that middle leaders are focusing on their people and starting to think through how they can develop them.

You can start with a simple team check-in and listen to what they say. You will usually get a good sense of who is a "safe pair of hands" and who they are working more to develop and how you can support this work.

It is a decent idea to sense-check this, however: make sure you both have the same idea of what we're aiming for in terms of great teaching. Taking time, particularly at the start of the year or the line management relationship, to walk the department and talk together about what you see lays the critical foundations for your shared work in the future. Try to do this periodically, and it need not be for long. Make sure there is a point to this venture: "let's go and check how Ellen is getting on – you said you think she's improved a huge amount." "I've not seen year 10 books actually – shall we walk around year 10 next Wednesday and take a particular look together at what we see?" "I can hear your concern around [whole-school initiative]; shall we see it in lessons together and think through what would work better?" In my experience, a sharp focus, ideally one that has come from your middle leader, works better than "let's go on a learning walk together!" when they have a long list of pressing matters they'd like to cover in their brief time with you.

In terms of what your line managee's list looks like, try to move on rapidly from anything admin-related. Ideally, establish a relationship where anything admin-related can be put in an email which you agree to action within a day. I've always felt the biggest waste of middle leader time is when they ask me something they'd already asked via email that is very easy to clarify by email but I didn't seem to manage to.

Put time aside to work on department meeting planning. This will ensure that you can foreground improving teacher subject practice and will allow your middle leader to understand what this might look like. You might marry this to whole-school objectives, but you might be led by them and what they are saying their needs are in the team: indeed, these needs might drive whole-school professional development in a different direction, and that's a great two-way conversation to be having.

Thinking about the benefits of foregrounding practice, try to ensure your middle leaders give over time in meetings to practice teaching (or, as in previous chapters, to practice planning). You want teachers to be doing the work in this time, not leaving a meeting with a massive to-do list. Aspects of practice that middle leaders might want their teams to work on include addressing misconceptions, explanations, modelling examples live, or questioning. These will be subject-specific and work best coming through departments, so support your middle leader to do the best job they can with these. Take a look at their meeting agenda together, particularly where department meetings are infrequent, and identify anything that is "admin" which can be either done through other channels or saved until last. (If you start with admin, it eats more time than you ever thought possible; keep it to the last five minutes and magically it doesn't spark needless further conversation.)

## Developing your middle leaders through line management

I once had a prospective middle leader ask when discussing their application for a role: "How will you develop me?" I thought it was an odd question, partly because I'd had only ten minutes to chat to them and I had no idea what their areas of development were (and they weren't likely to flag these prior to interview anyway). I also thought it was odd because the question seemed to require a simple answer, like "put you on a course." But the best development I've had as a middle leader and as a senior leader has been line management. I'm not sure my best line managers knew it, but every week was an opportunity to learn up close with them how they did things: how they thought, how they approached problems, how they solved them.

So, for senior leaders, the way you plan and run your time with middle leaders is absolutely crucial to their development in role.

We rarely have enough time with the people we manage, and leaders can become blockers to action. That's why it makes sense to check what is top of people's minds first – what is "on their list." It doesn't mean you'll cover it all, but you should probably cover the "top of mind" stuff, and you should assure people you're going to get back to them about everything they've said is important, so they don't spend the rest of your meeting with that in their heads.

Ideally, have a shared agenda. I have mixed feelings about these, because although theoretically these are a great way to check in on what your middle leaders want to cover prior to the meeting, as well as a great way to collect actions and RAG (red: not progressing; amber: on track; green: complete) them to save time going through them, I've never actually gotten people in the habit of doing this – no one seemed to have the time to do this before meetings, so I ended up losing the first seven minutes while they found the agenda and added to it, so it felt more like a paperwork exercise. That said, if you can get people into the habit of doing this, it should be a time-saver in the long term.

Action lists are critical. The most efficient line manager I had, the one who always got stuff done and ensured that I did as well, started every meeting rattling through the list to tick things off (or not). Anything not done, she'd fix me with a look and say "when can you do that?" and then stick a date by it. This is also really good to do because you can judge someone's workload and ability to do the needed job by the number of actions not done. Once that list creeps to ten things not done, you can pause the rest of the meeting and have a serious chat about workload and what's not working for that person or about prioritising. When the list is reasonable but one action seems not to be going anywhere (something we've all experienced; inexplicably, I like to call them "white whale actions"), you, as a senior leader, need to ask: "How can I help?"

The best use of your time together, though, is not in action checking and holding to account – it is in designing and practising the work they will do to develop their teams. It is hard to remember but important to do: if teacher quality is the thing that matters most for pupil outcomes, we need to spend most of our time thinking about how we develop teachers. Simple but hard – like most things in education.

Things you should be spending time doing together include scripting and practising tough meetings, perhaps where they need to hold others to account or where they need to pitch something to their teams and take their feedback, and professional development they want to deliver with their team. The more of the meeting that feels developmental, the better. Try to automate as many systems as you can for action checks and admin.

---

### Debbie Tremble, Assistant Headteacher (Teaching and Learning) at John Taylor High School and Evidence Lead in Education for Staffordshire Research School, shares her approach to developing middle leaders

*I'm sure we have all heard the analogy that "middle leaders are the engine room of the school." While that may be true, I, for one, was hugely unprepared for the role. When I became a middle leader, there were no national professional qualifications (NPQs) supporting professional development, and even today, with the availability of these courses, there will be many middle leaders who not yet have had the opportunity to pursue them.*

In education, this seems to be how it goes: a successful classroom teacher, perhaps with some small-scale experience of leading others, gets promoted to middle leadership. But where is the preparation for this undertaking? My experience as a middle leader taught me many valuable lessons, but my biggest takeaway was this: middle leaders need more than a fortnightly line management meeting where they are given a list of things to do. They need structure, guidance, and professional development alongside accountability.

Once I became an Assistant Headteacher and line managed middle leaders, I always had my own feeling of unpreparedness in the back of my mind. I was, therefore, empathetic to those "stuck in the middle" with competing demands for their time and energy. It wasn't until last year, however, that I was more proactive than empathetic.

The Headteacher at my school had restructured middle leadership, creating faculty leaders who oversaw not only their subject but also led other areas. The change came into effect just as I started. These faculty leaders varied in experience, and for some, this was their first leadership position. I came into the school as Assistant Headteacher for teaching and learning and PD; I was also tasked with line managing the middle leaders alongside the Head and deputies.

When designing PD for the faculty leads, I was mindful of varying levels of experience amongst the team. We had faculty leaders who were learning the ropes and others who had been in similar positions for years. Despite this, I knew it was important to design PD from the starting point of tackling the school's persistent problems. For novice leaders, support was given, and they were paired with more experienced leaders who had the mental models in place already. For example, as a school, we were looking to develop key stage 5 schemes of learning. I did not assume that all leaders had prior knowledge about curriculum design. Therefore, we worked collaboratively, bringing in expertise from the team to decide how to structure the scheme of learning template. This approach not only provided a professional development opportunity but also meant the middle leaders had ownership over the new schemes and felt much more empowered when delivering the concept to their teams. Other examples of PD included training on pupil book study, formative assessments, lesson observation training, and metacognition.

## Coaching

During the pandemic, I undertook a coaching certification. I saw this as a way to strengthen my practice as a leader. One of my main takeaways from coaching was that the person you are coaching is whole and capable, and they have the answers already. Middle leaders are possibly our busiest staff members in school, and this can make it difficult to see the wood for the trees. Therefore, I aim to bring coaching into our faculty leader meetings as often as possible to give them the time and space to strategise.

### Creating Cultures

*Last year, for the first time, we involved all middle leaders in the whole-school improvement plan. After our Headteacher delivered training to the middle leaders on successful implementation, we were put into working parties, where we reviewed distinct areas of the previous year's plan and conducted a strengths/weaknesses/opportunities/threats (SWOT) analysis. We then decided on the active ingredients together, and through this co-creation of the school improvement plan, middle leaders had far more ownership of it and, therefore, more buy-in when enacting the plan. We often talk about the school as a whole and emphasize that we are not responsible for our own subjects and teams; we are a collective. We celebrate the wins together, encourage each other, share best practice, and collaborate.*

## Key takeaways

- Professional development is a crucial tool for faculty leaders, tailored to varying levels of experience.

- Coaching empowers middle leaders, who are capable individuals who may just need guidance and support to see the bigger picture.

- The creation of a collaborative culture among middle leaders is a driving force for school improvement.

- Celebrating wins, sharing best practice, and fostering a sense of unity contribute to a more dynamic and effective middle leadership team.

## Monitoring and evaluation

I didn't even know what self-evaluation was when I took on my first Head of Department role. My boss asked me what I thought it was (a classic 2000s teacher question), and I replied "Is it where I think about how good I am at stuff?" He laughed and then showed me a massive lever-arch folder he'd compiled in role with the title "self-evaluation." In my mind, the term has never quite extricated itself from that massive lever-arch folder.

Self-evaluation so often becomes about form filling, and we need to work really hard to make that not the case. If we want to determine whether teaching is improving, we clearly need to evaluate it and monitor it. But I've worked in too many schools with too many Excel sheets, Microsoft forms, and lever-arch files to think that documenting what you see is the way you monitor it and check its effectiveness.

Even the biggest schools aren't very big. I've worked in 700 pupil schools and 1800 pupil schools, and in both you could walk every corridor in 30 minutes. There are some odd anomalies of architecture, but at worst you might need an hour to walk an entire school building.

What I'm trying to say is you shouldn't need to look at pieces of paper or spread-sheets to know what is going on in the school you are leading. You should carve out the time to walk it, ideally every day but certainly twice a week. If you're a Headteacher, that means the whole of it; if you're a senior leader, that needs to be only the part of it you manage – and if you're a pastoral leaders, you can walk the whole school in chunks across the week, focusing on either year groups or geographical parts of the site.

One of the most powerful things we can do as leaders is walk around schools with the right people. At Success Academies, school principals start the year with joint walk-throughs of all classrooms: "We're going to start by going in, observing, then pop out of the room. What did you see? I want to see that you're noticing the same things I'm noticing."[9] This is so powerful because leaders rapidly develop a shared sense of what they are all aiming for in their work. Further, this can be done with your middle leaders, and the conversations and actions that come out of this work are far more purposeful, I would argue, than the folder of proof. (And in support of that lever-arch folder, compiled by one of the most inspiring and effective senior leaders I've ever had the privilege to work for, this was a time when Ofsted most certainly would have been interested to see it. We are blessed to no longer live in such a time of accountability where paper outweighs what is seen with inspectors' eyes.)

You should also spend time periodically looking at work in pupils' books. This is important for senior leaders, but it is particularly important for those with subject-specific expertise. That is because understanding what you're seeing in pupil books is incredibly tough when you're not a subject expert. I vividly remember looking at pupil books with a Maths expert, who pointed out that, although there was a vast amount of pupil practice and green pen self-corrections, all neatly and beautifully kept, the work was inappropriately pitched for the age and stage of those pupils. Similarly, I've pointed out to others that a perfect-looking paragraph is indeed just that: it's the model paragraph, and I know that because I've also taught that lesson with that model paragraph on slide 11.

We should not overestimate what we can get from looking at pupil books, and we should certainly do our looking with a subject expert, ideally the Head of Department, who can narrate what we are seeing with precision (hopefully). The most impactful book looking, in my experience, is that done at whole-department level, where everyone brings the books of a particular year group and you swap and look. This threw up some interesting points, such as "set 3 are writing much better than set 2! How are you doing it?" It really allowed us to share some great practice and shine a light on bright spots as well as to identify places in the curriculum where we needed to collectively strengthen our planning.

The other aspect of self-evaluation that gets a lot of leaders' time sunk into it is data reviews. As we've covered earlier in our discussion of assessment, spend far less time on this. After national exams, ensure that Heads of Department are reviewing marks across units to check if the department's teaching of any particular unit could do with an overhaul. I'd suggest only looking for broad-brush feedback here – one or two pupils doing unexpectedly poorly in one paper or question is likely to be chance, but if a significant proportion of an entire year group scores below national average for one particular element, it signals a curriculum weakness you'll want to address.

What other data is worth looking at for senior and middle leaders? I've worked in schools that invested a lot in nationally standardised reading tests such as the New Group Reading Test (NGRT). In my experience, data of this kind can show you at a whole-school level where your weak spots are (year 8 seeming particularly far behind, for example), but it's almost pointless at pupil level. You'll look down the list of outliers and find pupils who you know read proficiently scoring below expectations and pupils who struggle magically making 24 months' progress. But what is significant, again, is cohort progress: if, by and large, your NGRT results are better this year than last year for the same group of pupils, something is probably working in your curriculum.

There are other standardised tests you could consider giving year groups annually, though it is worth bearing in mind that if your curriculum isn't geared towards success in these (and I don't think it should be), poor performance comparably could signal either that your curriculum is weak or that other schools' curricula map more readily onto those tests. I think they're a decent sense-check, but again not necessarily something you'll be wanting to choose to invest quite so much time and money in, and if you do, know that it is as a sense-check and not something you'll want people to do a deep dive into.

Internal subject assessment data is hard to gauge, even in large MATs with MAT-standardised tests. Creating assessments that are valid and reliable enough to make decisions based on the data is incredibly hard (as discussed in the previous chapter), so spend time analysing this with a large dose of caution. At best, with school or MAT-level tests, you can probably see large differences between teachers and classes and know where to do some more digging to find other data to confirm or deny your data-based speculations.

On balance, I think we probably need to spend far less time looking at data and filling in forms and far more time inside classrooms, thinking about how we can get our curriculum, behaviour, and teaching better. Focus on that, and results will take care of themselves.

---

### Tracey O'Brien, Headteacher at Wallington High School for Girls in Sutton, London, writes about developing a more empowering approach to quality assurance

*There was a time when I had folders for everything. Folders of lesson observations, learning walks, book looks, outcomes, meeting notes, department review documents, tutor time observations, student surveys, staff surveys... and more. I collected everything, I read everything, I knew everything - or so I thought.*

*What, in fact, I knew, was what I wanted to know. So heavily contrived and planned, all these quality assurance activities were actually designed for me.*

*So that I could be secure in my role when it came to planning CPD, or design-*
*ing a Teaching and learning action plan, or for when Ofsted came.*

*Over time I realised that I didn't actually need to know all this stuff. I needed*
*to know processes were in place for staff to know really well what was going on*
*in their areas, but that it didn't have to be me sitting on all this detail across the*
*whole school. I realised I could pass on this responsibility to the other profes-*
*sionals in the school and that I needed a different mechanism to review school*
*life and that actually I needed to replace "quality assurance" with "self-review."*

*Learning to trust others, to delegate, to listen more. These were not easy to*
*start with, and as a relatively young school leader (at the time) I certainly felt my*
*fair share of imposter syndrome, but I knew I had to let go and lose the folders.*

*I read a great deal about self-review, system leadership, and self-improving*
*systems, and over a year or so put all my new knowledge and thinking into my*
*own whole-school self-review approach. Instead of collecting evidence about*
*everything I designed self-review activities solely around the school priorities.*
*Reading the work of John Tomsett and David Didau, I empowered team lead-*
*ers to review their own priorities that sat underneath the whole-school ones.*

*I created an annual calendar called the school Self Review Schedule (SRS),*
*carefully mapping different review activities across the year. Learning walks*
*to check how year 7 and 12 had settled in at the start of October, student*
*voice with year 11 after their mocks to find out about their study skills and*
*how effective they had been, and then adding in other activities based on our*
*own priorities such as a SEN review bringing in other practitioners to help*
*quality-assure our own processes and add value and knowledge from outside.*

*Subject reviews moved away from huge deep dives into more focused*
*reviews on what the department was working on themselves – their priorities*
*already having been set at the start of the year – aligning to the school's devel-*
*opment priorities and looked at rigorously at SLT level. I am a great believer*
*in the power of peer review, so I ensured peer review was just that. It was not*
*a done-to activity by people from outside who came in to tell us what to do –*
*rather it was matching my teams up with teams from other schools where*
*practice was discussed and ideas were shared.*

*Overall, there was a reduction in workload across all levels, staff felt more*
*trusted and we created time to focus on other things, not just quality assur-*
*ance for the sake of it.*

## Teaching SEND pupils

Before we begin, I will say again that not all special educational needs and disa-
bility (SEND) correlates to poor academic performance. Some children with SEND
achieve in line with national expectations or above. National data, however, show

that the depressingly large majority of pupils with additional or special educational needs dramatically underperform in terms of their educational outcomes: in 2021/22, for example, 22.5% of pupils with SEND support achieved a grade 5 in English and Maths at General Certificate of Secondary Education (GCSE) compared with 55.8% of pupils with no SEND needs. For pupils with an Education, Health and Care Plan (EHCP), this number was 7%. Over recent years, with the increase in pupils identified as having a special educational need and special schools full to the brim, schools have had to cope with increasingly diverse bodies of pupils, not all of whom can readily access the curriculum in the ways of their counterparts. Schools have become increasingly concerned with how they can better meet the needs of these young people, and rightly so.

I've argued in the previous chapter that children with SEND benefit from a rigorous academic curriculum, albeit one which prioritises depth over breadth to ensure they can master some of it and, ultimately, leave with some outcomes that open doors and give them the possibility of choice in their careers and lives.

So, how can we best lead the teaching of children with SEND?

"Adaptive teaching," education's latest buzzword, cannot become differentiation in another guise. Differentiation used to mean planning for pupils who were low-attaining, many of whom also had complex SEND needs. In effect, teachers would plan whole different objectives and worksheets, preventing SEND pupils from accessing the richness and depth of the curriculum, as well as ensuring they ploughed this furrow without the guidance of the expert in the room: while the teacher taught the class, the individual would work through easy work on their own or with a teaching assistant, who was almost never a trained teacher or subject expert. It is easy to see how such an approach becomes harmful for those most in need of teacher instruction.

Despite the often complex needs present in today's classrooms, it is still worth bearing in mind that even children at wildly different ends of the ability and need spectrum largely learn in the same way: by having material presented to them in a clear way, in manageable chunks, being asked questions and set exercises to ensure they understand that material and are able to do something with it, and being asked about it after a few days, weeks, months, and years to check they've remembered it.

The other critical aspect about teaching SEND pupils is that much of what particularly benefits pupils with SEND will also benefit the non-SEND pupils in your classroom (which is very unlike the old approach of essentially planning and teaching multiple versions of lessons at the same time, which benefitted no one and was certainly harmful to some).

The EEF's report on SEND underlines this: the strategies that report advocates for are all aspects that benefit all pupils in your classroom. Explicit instruction has been shown to be beneficial to all pupils. Managing pupil cognitive load will be helpful to all pupils' learning, not just those with SEND. In fact, every other aspect in this report is a helpful addition to teachers who have zero pupils with SEND in their classroom: giving children opportunities to plan, monitor, and evaluate their learning, providing scaffolding such as a writing frame or exemplar and removing this as pupils improve over time, flexible grouping based on a curriculum need rather than fixed as a general ability, and using technology like visualisers.[10]

There will be occasions where a particular pupil does require something quite specific. I've worked with deaf pupils who must be sat at the front to best lip-read, for example, and who will need other specific supports depending on their particular needs. Whatever those needs, we should definitely ensure that we are knowledgeable about the very specific strategies we will need teachers to employ with particular pupils. As leaders, we should be checking that classrooms are meeting all needs, but particularly paying attention to the most vulnerable learners, and feeding back to teachers where they could better meet those needs particularly within their classroom, and not by planning additional or separate activities or worksheets.

### Adam Rowe, Assistant Principal (Teaching and Learning & SENDCO) at Houstone School, part of Advantage Schools, in Houghton Regis, outlines his school's approach to teaching pupils with SEND

*At Houstone, we believe, given the right circumstances, all children are capable of extraordinary things. This is our driving force behind our approach to teaching pupils with SEND. The way that we make this happen is through "quality-first teaching" and not doing anything unnecessarily radically different. Houstone exists to raise the expectations of children, families and the town more widely, especially those most vulnerable and those with SEND. We try to distil and simplify what helps pupils with SEND to learn in the best way possible. I will discuss how booklets, re-thinking differentiation and providing the right support to staff can ensure pupils with SEND succeed.*

#### Booklets

*We know that pupils with SEND learn far more similarly than differently to those without SEND, and we know what ensures pupils make progress. Although we say "subject is king," which means heads of department ultimately get to choose how they deliver their curriculum, we strongly encourage the use of booklets to deliver a subject's curriculum.*

*Using booklets provides a great structure for how to deliver new knowledge. Every booklet contains retrieval practice "Do Now" activities, lots of reading to explain new concepts and to get pupils practising reading generally, and reading subject-specific terminology. They contain lots of examples, non-examples and models. They contain diagrams and images to support explanations, contain the tasks and writing space to complete work, so that everything is in one place. The booklets also contain page numbers and line numbers to more easily allow pupils to follow the reading and not lose track.*

*The teacher then uses the booklet, under a visualiser, as their primary resource to teach from. This removes any chance of split attention across an unnecessarily animated and cognitively overloading PowerPoint, exercise book and multiple worksheets. We think that doing all of these things, along with using models, checking for understanding and precise explanation over and over again, will solve most of the barriers that pupils with SEND face.*

### Differentiation

*We know, however, that some pupils sometimes need something a little bit different to their peers. A common misconception with having a booklet curriculum is that "the booklet is the lesson." At Houstone, we make it extremely clear that this is not the case and that the booklet is just the best tool the teacher has to support their delivery of new knowledge. Teachers are told to ditch what they knew about differentiation, and that it is morally wrong to cap what a child should know because they happen to be on the SEND register. Teachers are trained in adaptive teaching and knowing the reasonable adjustments to their lessons which will remove the barriers certain children have to learning. This might be some non-verbal cues for children struggling with focus, a sentence starter or some key words to get started or use of the seating plan. It is the small things that remove barriers and ensure all pupils are able to work towards achieving the same lesson outcome, rather than creating three different resources and limiting what pupils can achieve.*

### Support for staff

*Even then, we know that some pupils can present with significant challenges that might require more support than reasonable adjustments. To prepare teachers to teach these pupils, the special educational needs co-ordinator (SENCO) will deliver a briefing covering the key strategies as outlined in a pupil's Learning Passport (also known as an IEP) or Mini EHCP. A Learning Passport is a document for pupils who do not have an EHCP that outlines the barriers they face, and the best techniques that can be used to resolve them. The Mini EHCP fulfils a similar role, but also briefly outlines what a lengthy EHCP states the school should do to support the child. The strategies will have come from meeting the child, parent or carer, and a round robin of teachers. There may also be additional adult support to help the child, although we always try and avoid pairing up a child up one-to-one with a teaching assistant to reduce the possibility of social exclusion and over-reliance. There will occasionally be whole-staff CPD sessions on particular children, where we go over how best to support these pupils. Every week in morning staff briefing, one or two Learning Passports or Mini EHCPs are shared with staff as a reminder for staff to prevent information overload.*

> *All of this work is made possible by teachers being trained effectively through inset, weekly CPD and staff briefing, and the specific training SEND staff undertake. At Houstone, the SENCO is also the person in charge of teaching and learning, because we know that what helps SEND pupils succeed is great teaching. The SENCO is then supported by an Assistant SENCO, who is not a teacher, and who runs the day-to-day of SEND in the school such as meeting parents, completing paperwork and supporting pupils in crisis.*
>
> *Ultimately, pupils with SEND will be successful if teachers consistently do what we know makes children learn day in, day out.*

## Teaching pupils with English as an additional language

Again, this is one of those challenges that are more prevalent in some schools than others. Much of your success with English as an Additional Language (EAL) learners is predicated on their literacy in their home language and the similarity of that language and alphabet to English. For learners who can read and write at around the usual level expected of a child their age, their language acquisition will normally be rapid the more they are immersed in it. In that way, ensuring that they hear great examples of spoken English is really important. Of course, they will need additional support to access work and access to a dictionary they can use to translate key vocabulary to their home language. In the very early stages, they might write in their home language for extended pieces.

## Key takeaways

- Build practice into professional development to make embedding improvements more likely.

- Give teachers time to embed new practices.

- Walk with your middle leaders to create a shared understanding of teaching practice.

- Be suspicious of anyone who tells you data or documents are the route to understanding teaching quality.

Although the past three chapters have been by no means exhaustive on the critical triad of behaviour, curriculum, and teaching, I hope they have provided some useful guidance and examples for leaders and aspirant leaders to employ in their settings. Our final chapter turns the focus to that other key aspect of schooling: school operations.

# Notes

1 The EEF's 2021 report on professional development states: "No matter the phase or school setting, it is the quality of teaching that can make the biggest difference to children's learning and to their ultimate success in school. As Rauch and Coe explain, it is 'arguably the single most important thing that teachers and school leaders can focus on to make a difference in children's learning'. What's more, the quality of teaching is not fixed: teachers can be improved, and they can be improved via effective professional development" (EEF, 2021).
2 Dylan Wiliam, SSAT conference speech, 2012.
3 Peps McCrea *Developing Expert Teaching* 2023 p. 10.
4 Doug Lemov *Teach Like a Champion 3.0* Jossey Bass 2021.
5 Paul Bambrick-Santoyo *Leverage Leadership* Jossey Bass 2012 p. 61.
6 Dr Sam Sims has helpfully catalogued the array of meta-analyses that show the positive impact of instructional coaching here: https://samsims.education/2019/02/19/247/.
7 As taken from *Leverage Leadership* Paul Bambrick-Santoyo (Jossey Bass 2018).
8 Sims, S., Fletcher-Wood, H., O'Mara-Eves, A., Cottingham, S., Stansfield, C., Van Herwegen, J., Anders, J. *What are the Characteristics of Teacher Professional Development that Increase Pupil Achievement? A systematic review and meta-analysis.* London: Education.

   Endowment Foundation (2021); S. Sims, H. Fletcher-Wood, A. O'Mara-Eves, S. Cottingham, C. Stansfield, J. Goodrich, J. Van Herwegen, J. Anders (2022). Effective teacher professional development: new theory and a meta-analytic test. (EdWorkingPaper: 22-507). Retrieved from Annenberg Institute at Brown University: https://doi.org/10.26300/rzet-bf74.
9 Robert Pondiscio *How the Other Half Learns* Avery 2019 p. 23.
10 https://d2tic4wvo1iusb.cloudfront.net/production/eef-guidance-reports/send/EEF_Special_Educational_Needs_in_Mainstream_Schools_Guidance_Report.pdf?v=1690702490.

# 4 The operational running of schools

I've long been a fan of simplicity and have definitely been heard to say in the past that the only things that matter in running schools are curriculum, teaching, and behaviour. But that is incorrect. The miscellany of running schools is something I've been more and more exposed to the further "up" in leadership I've travelled, and few education books tackle this.

This chapter is a "making the trains run on time" or rather "making sure every pupil has a chair" kind of thing: absolutely essential but not often the subject of education books. We'll look at how to structure the school day, managing timetables as well as breaks, canteens and exams, duties and reporting, governance and administration, working with colleagues, meetings, as well as compliance around key aspects of leadership.

## The shape of the school day

This is the first building block of a school and might seem like an immovable foundation. It is not. In fact, in the majority of schools I've worked in, the leadership have changed the school day during, just before, or just after I've worked there. Before we dive into this, I'll be clear that this is an operational concern that chiefly impacts secondary colleagues: for primary colleagues, there will be some shared considerations around timetabling which we'll look at later in this chapter, but as the majority of primary schools operate with one main class teacher, the length of lessons will be determined largely by that teacher or their year or phase leader. These lesson lengths are likely to be determined by the curriculum content and the age and stage of the pupils more than any whole-school building blocks.

For secondary colleagues who know change is needed in the shape of the school day, this can feel terrifyingly big, but as long as you have consulted with your union representatives and then the wider staff body, the pupils and then their parents, it is eminently do-able.

DOI: 10.4324/9781003465461-5

Unless your canteen and outdoor spaces are genuinely too tiny, I'd always advocate having break and lunch time be the same time for everyone. This is because it is very challenging for teachers to hold in their heads multiple differing lesson times, and it is almost impossible to get children to concentrate in lessons when the very exciting sounds of "first lunch" are right outside the window. Similarly, go for simplicity on lesson length: it is wildly irritating to remember that period four is always five minutes shorter, for example. Simplicity in timings and lesson lengths is a key first ingredient.

I can't find any research on the shape of the school day, but in a secondary school context, I'd personally advocate six 60-minute periods, split into two – break – two – lunch – two – home. You might have 50- or 55-minute lessons if you're looking to put more tutor time in there. Lunch should be as close to 30 minutes as you can push everyone through the canteen (which normally makes it closer to an hour), and break should be as close to 30 minutes as you can make it – though it is likely to be more like 20 – so everyone can get food, use the bathroom, and have a decent run-around.

The amount of time your pupils spend with tutors is something to be carefully thought through. Ideally, I'd bookend the day with tutor time – probably one 15 minutes and one closer to 30, and I'd run a reading programme in one of them so children read for pleasure as a full class. Fifteen minutes is extremely challenging time-wise, but I'd make one half of tutor time as short as it can be to register everyone and give them a quick pep talk for the day, and the other I'd make all about reading. If you have a million notices that tutors need to get through, I'd suggest there are other factors overcomplicating the running of the school to think through rather than immediately increasing tutor time. That said, in a very large building, if you run a line-up, you will be able to see how long it genuinely takes pupils to make it into classrooms, and you can adjust your timings accordingly.

In the best-run schools, tutor time can be quick and efficient as well as purposeful. I've heard of schools where pupils are reading in their 15-minute slot, having got their books and equipment out during five minutes of line-up, and getting through the door and immediately beginning, with the tutor registering while another pupil reads aloud for the class. It is seeing such miracles of efficiency that brings to life the notion that every minute of school time is precious and worth using well.

Indeed, using every minute of time well is key to running a great school, and this goes for all aspects of the structure of the school day. Think through when and how line-ups will be used and practice these until they take two minutes. Even in very large buildings, I've seen 900 pupils silent, spoken to, and cleared out of the playground in two minutes. It is absolutely possible.

# Timetables

Getting the timetable right feels like one of those Sisyphean tasks, and it goes without saying that you will never have the perfect timetable. Any timetable requires some degree of compromise. Leaders must be confident about their priorities going into timetable writing, in order that the inevitable compromises are not damaging their curriculum priorities and aims for outcomes.

While the challenge for primary leaders around timetabling is more logistical – ensuring that key resources like the hall, computer room, and physical education (PE) facilities are used at the optimal times by different classes and that planning, preparation, and assessment (PPA) is allocated sensibly, along with managing staffing for shared elements such as a specialist teacher or for phonics groups – timetabling is arguably a more complex beast for secondary leaders, and so this section will be focused on that context.

I've found it helpful to list these principles in order of importance, so the leader making the timetable knows which can absolutely not break, and so they can attempt to create a timetable that mitigates these.

I present my own principles here as an example, in the full knowledge that these will map to almost no one else's – your principles and your school priorities are likely to be different.

i   No split classes

For me, this was always the top priority because I felt the relationship between the teacher and the class was key, and the logistics of ensuring teaching and curriculum coherence are much more challenging across multiple teachers. Although there would be circumstances of inevitable class-sharing with some teachers working part-time, any teacher of a core subject (of which there were five periods a week) who worked five days would not share a class, and teachers of subjects where the number of periods a week corresponded to the days worked would also not share; that is, if we had three periods of History a week and my History teacher worked three days a week, they would not share a class.

The exception to this was where teachers worked three or two days a week, and their subject had more periods. For example, I had an English teacher (five periods a week of English) working three days. This meant inevitably that her classes would be split ones. If you think it would be better to block English and have double periods, firstly this conflicts with my third principle (see below), but also if the majority of teachers are full-time, I felt like this would compromise two of my top three principles to meet the first.

ii  Single periods only, except for PE

For me, memory is a key element in learning, and the ability to get pupils to remember prior learning is important. Another key element is working memory and not overloading it. In a double period, say around 100 to 120 minutes, I think it is very easy to overload working memory and therefore very tempting to do "easy" work for lots of this time and thus not covering the curriculum in an efficient manner. With single periods, particularly with subjects where teachers see pupils for only two or three periods a week, you have more opportunities to revisit prior knowledge and chunk new learning. In General Certificate of Secondary Education (GCSE) options subjects, I've worked in schools which run a double and a single, giving pupils only two times a week to revisit prior knowledge and work through the curriculum. In addition, if a pupil happens to be absent on the double-period day, they've missed two thirds of their curriculum provision that week, and it will be incredibly hard for them to catch up.

My exception is PE, because I've never managed to get pupils changed in and out of PE kit fast enough, and I've also worked in schools where bus transfer to PE facilities was required – something depressingly common in inner city schools. In my dream school, the one I've never managed to run, I'd make pupils wear tracksuits as their uniform so they could transition smoothly from classrooms to the sports pitch and back. If that were the case, I'd probably make PE a single period as well, because surely exercising across the week is better than blocking it in one go.

iii Lessons spread across the week

Again, to support all pupils in revisiting prior knowledge and converting it to long-term memory, I think it's important to maximise the number of times pupils have exposure to that subject and opportunities to retrieve prior knowledge. Therefore, in addition to single periods, I'd prioritise having those periods spread evenly across the week. For example, it's better to have Maths daily than two periods on a Tuesday, even if they are split across the day (e.g. periods 1 and 5). Similarly, it's rather have Music Monday and Thursday than Monday and Tuesday, because the gaps between Wednesday and the following Monday feel extremely long to not be thinking about the subject at all.

iv Strongest teachers with weakest groups

When it comes to teacher allocation, I would try to prioritise the children who find learning most challenging. These groups are most complex to teach, so it's important they get a great deal. Because you don't necessarily want your strongest teachers teaching only one ability stream, I'd prioritise year 7 for this in the hopes of ensuring a most effective catch-up. For sure, though, I'd aim to have no weak groups with trainee teachers. They just don't have the skills developed yet to manage these groups' learning well, and pupils in low-attaining groups don't have even five minutes to spare in a learning year.

v  Keep teachers with groups

In my experience, even with weaker teachers, children tend to do better when they know the teacher. That's because teaching is not just about learning curriculum and techniques, it is also about building strong relationships. Unless the relationship the previous year has somehow gone badly wrong, I'd keep groups with the same teacher. Even if it wasn't wildly successful, it is more likely to become so where relationships are established. (I vividly remember one year 10, whom I'd taught the previous year as a trainee teacher, saying "Miss, you can teach this year," which was both heart-breaking and true. What I felt at the time was that the class had changed just as much as I had; I'd certainly not become a decent teacher over the summer holiday. They'd just come back and knew what to expect, and so did I.)

vi  Year 11 Maths in the morning

Like most leaders, I try to balance the long-term learning of all pupils in all subjects with the urgent need for exam classes to do well in the subjects most important to opening doors in the future. In my experience, Maths has tended to be the limiting factor for pupils in achieving their next steps, and so where possible I'd put Maths in the morning for Year 11, when they tend to be fresher and more focused – in my experience.

vii  Year 11 English in the morning

For the same reasons as above, I'd put English in the morning; it's a lower priority because I've tended to find that pupils are doing better in this subject in Year 11.

viii Lower-attaining groups Maths in the morning

As a final "wish list" for the timetabling teacher, I'd want any groups low achieving in Maths to learn in the morning, again when they are fresher for learning.

You are likely to disagree with some of these principles or maybe all – maybe these don't map at all to your experiences and your school context. What is important is that you carefully think through the guiding principles for your timetable, in the knowledge that not all of these will be possible, so you are sure you know what you're ready to compromise on.

In terms of the physical writing of the timetable, I'll leave that to Sarah Warnock to share.

### Sarah Warnock, Assistant Headteacher at Priory Pembroke Academy, shares her approach to timetabling in an 11–16 school

*The process below is used to create a timetable for an 11–16 school, however the concepts can be adapted to work in all secondary settings. Involving subject leaders at all stages is key to a successful timetable. Keep a separate notebook or file for timetabling. Notes made across the year are easier to track this way*

#### Term 1

- *Watch the new timetable in action. Note:*
  - *Flow of the timetable;*
  - *Pinch points;*
- *Review with Subject Leads:*
  - *What works well;*
  - *Things to improve;*
  - *Things to avoid.*
  - *Discuss curriculum changes for the next academic year:*
    - *Subjects for KS4 options,*
    - *Staffing needs and resourcing*
  - *Update curriculum models with current timetable and projected student numbers. Aim for 5-year planning.*
- *Timetable meeting with Headteacher (this should be a termly meeting):*
  - *Staffing and resourcing for the coming year(s);*
  - *issues identified and possible solutions;*

#### Term 2

- *Survey students: initial thoughts for KS4 options. Gain information on:*
  - *Viability of subjects*
  - *Potential number of groups*
  - *Staffing gaps*

- *Meet with Subject Leaders to discuss survey and finalise KS4 offer.*
- *Termly meeting with Headteacher, as above with updates*

### Term 3

- *Start KS4 Options process*
- *Meet with Subject Leaders to create timetable "wish list." These requests are not guaranteed:*
  - ❏ *Staff/group allocations*
  - ❏ *Subject rotations*
  - ❏ *Rooming*
  - ❏ *Other considerations (e.g. additional responsibilities such as Early Career Teacher mentoring)*
- *Termly meeting with Headteacher*

### Term 4

- *Timetable preparation*
  - ❏ *Staff allocations*
    - ❏ *Confirm working days for part-time staff*
    - ❏ *Adjust teaching allocation for any Teaching and Learning Responsibilities, mentoring time, part-time, and so on*
  - ❏ *Room allocations*
    - ❏ *Consider limitations, such as number of science labs or computer rooms*
  - ❏ *Model known "blocks," including KS4 options.*
- *Termly meeting with Headteacher*

### Term 5

*Building the timetable (I timetable manually using Microsoft Excel). Be prepared to repeat this process several times until you are happy!*

- *Block out days for part time staff*
- *Add option blocks and rotations that limit other subjects and staffing*
- *Timetable core subjects for KS4 then KS3*

- *Add staff and rooms*
- *Review the timetable*
  - ❏ *Look for balance – subjects should have a fair split between morning and afternoon lessons*
  - ❏ *Check for double lessons across a day, e.g. Science and Triple Science, or two subjects with same teacher*
  - ❏ *Check room availability, especially computer rooms, labs, and workshops*
  - ❏ *Check staff allocations – are they already timetabled? Do they have the required hours available?*
  - ❏ *Look for allocation balance between teachers of a subject – don't have one teacher at full timetable and another at 50%*
  - ❏ *Check for split classes – avoid this as far as possible*
  - ❏ *Keep room changes for staff to a minimum across the day. Where necessary, try for changes over break times.*
  - ❏ *Check PPA – spread across the week is usually better for staff wellbeing.*
- *Adjust the timetable and repeat the review*
- *Review with Senior Leadership Team (SLT) and adjust the timetable*
- *Review with Subject Leaders and adjust the timetable*
  - ❏ *Subject Leaders to begin producing class lists*
- *Termly meeting with Headteacher*

### Term 6

- *Confirm staffing after the May resignation deadline*
- *Complete final review*
- *Input to Information Management System (e.g. SIMS) if timetable is built in Excel or a timetabling program*
- *Share timetables with staff with time to make adjustments if issues are raised.*
- *Termly meeting with Headteacher*

| 2024/25 | | Subject | Maths | English | Science | Life | RE | Computing | PE | D&T | Food | History | Geog | Languages | Art | Drama | Music | PE Option | Triple Science | Photography | Statistics | Citizenship | Intervention | Business | Media | Reading | Check & Balance | |
|---|---|---|---|---|---|---|---|---|---|---|---|---|---|---|---|---|---|---|---|---|---|---|---|---|---|---|---|---|
| Y7 | 128 | pds | 3 | 3 | 3 | 1 | 1 | 1 | 2 | 1 | 0 | 2 | 2 | 2 | 1 | 1 | 1 | | | | | | | | | 1 | | |
| Y7 | | classes | 4 | 4 | 4 | 4 | 4 | 6 | 6 | 6 | 0 | 4 | 4 | 4 | 4 | 4 | 6 | | | | | | | | | 6 | | |
| Y7 | | extra | | | | | | | | | | | | | | | | | | | | | | | | | | |
| Y7 | | Total | 12 | 12 | 12 | 4 | 4 | 6 | 12 | 6 | 0 | 8 | 8 | 8 | 4 | 4 | 6 | 0 | 0 | 0 | 0 | 0 | 0 | | 0 | 6 | 112 | 112 |
| Y8 | 128 | pds | 3 | 3 | 3 | 1 | 1 | 1 | 2 | 1 | 0 | 2 | 2 | 2 | 1 | 1 | 1 | | | | | | | | | 1 | | |
| Y8 | | classes | 4 | 4 | 4 | 4 | 4 | | 6 | 6 | 0 | 4 | 4 | 4 | 4 | 4 | 6 | | | | | | | | | | | |
| Y8 | | extra | | | | | | 6 | | | | | | | | | | | | | | | | | | 6 | | |
| Y8 | | Total | 12 | 12 | 12 | 4 | 4 | 6 | 12 | 6 | 0 | 8 | 8 | 8 | 4 | 4 | 6 | 0 | 0 | 0 | 0 | 0 | 0 | | 0 | 6 | 112 | 112 |
| Y9 | 126 | pds | 3 | 4 | 4 | 1 | 1 | 1 | 2 | 1 | 0 | 2 | 2 | 2 | 1 | 1 | 1 | | | | | | | | 1 | 0 | | |
| Y9 | | classes | 4 | 4 | 4 | 4 | 4 | 4 | 6 | 8 | 0 | 4 | 4 | 4 | 2 | 2 | 2 | | | | | | | | 2 | 0 | | |
| Y9 | | extra | | | | | | | | | | | | | | | | | | | | | | | | | |
| Y9 | | Total | 12 | 16 | 16 | 4 | 4 | 4 | 12 | 8 | 0 | 8 | 8 | 8 | 2 | 2 | 2 | 0 | 0 | 0 | 0 | 0 | 0 | | 2 | 0 | 108 | 108 |
| KS3 | | Total | 36 | 40 | 40 | 12 | 12 | 16 | 36 | 20 | 0 | 24 | 24 | 24 | 10 | 10 | 14 | 0 | 0 | 0 | 0 | 0 | 0 | | 2 | 12 | | 332 |
| Y10 | 124 | pds | 4 | 4 | 4 | 1 | 2 | 3 | 1 | 3 | 3 | 3 | 3 | 3 | 3 | 3 | 2 | 3 | 3 | 3 | 2 | 2 | | 2 | 3 | 0 | | |
| Y10 | | classes | 4 | 4 | 4 | 4 | 1 | 1 | | 1 | 2 | 2 | 3 | 2 | 1 | 1 | 1 | | 1 | 1 | 1 | 1 | | 2 | 1 | 0 | | |
| Y10 | | ext/opt | | | | | | | 4 | | | | | | | | | 2 | | | | | | | | | | |
| Y10 | | Total | 16 | 16 | 16 | 4 | 2 | 3 | 4 | 3 | 6 | 6 | 9 | 6 | 3 | 3 | 2 | 6 | 3 | 3 | 2 | 2 | 0 | 4 | 3 | 0 | 122 | 122 |
| Y11 | 111 | pds | 4 | 4 | 4 | 1 | 2 | 3 | 1 | 3 | 3 | 3 | 3 | 3 | 3 | 3 | 2 | 3 | 3 | 3 | 2 | 2 | | 2 | 3 | 0 | | |
| Y11 | | classes | 4 | 4 | 4 | 4 | 1 | 1 | | 1 | 1 | 2 | 3 | 2 | 1 | 1 | 1 | | 1 | 1 | 1 | 1 | | 2 | 1 | 0 | | |
| Y11 | | ext/opt | | | | | | | 4 | | | | | | | | | 2 | | | | | | | | | | |
| Y11 | | Total | 16 | 16 | 16 | 4 | 2 | 3 | 4 | 3 | 3 | 6 | 9 | 6 | 3 | 3 | 2 | 6 | 3 | 3 | 2 | 2 | 0 | 4 | 3 | 0 | 119 | 119 |
| KS4 | | Total | 32 | 32 | 32 | 8 | 4 | 6 | 8 | 6 | 9 | 12 | 18 | 12 | 6 | 6 | 4 | 12 | 6 | 6 | 4 | 4 | 0 | 8 | 6 | 0 | | 241 |
| Total | | | 68 | 72 | 72 | 20 | 16 | 22 | 44 | 26 | 9 | 36 | 42 | 36 | 16 | 16 | 18 | 12 | 6 | 6 | 4 | 4 | 0 | 8 | 8 | 12 | | 573 |

**Figure 4.1** Aim for 5-year planning.

## Figure 4.2 — STAFF

| Subject | Available | Required | Difference |
|---|---|---|---|
| Reader Carousel | 12 | 12 | 0 |
| Media | 12 | 8 | 4 |
| Business | 8 | 4 | 4 |
| Intervention | 0 | 0 | 0 |
| Citizenship | 4 | 6 | -2 |
| Statistics | 6 | 6 | 0 |
| Photography | 6 | 6 | 0 |
| Triple Sci | 6 | 6 | 0 |
| PE Option | 9 | 9 | 0 |
| Music | 22 | 18 | 4 |
| Drama | 21 | 16 | 5 |
| Art | 16 | 16 | 0 |
| Spanish | 40 | 36 | 4 |
| Geog | 38 | 39 | -1 |
| History | 36 | 36 | 0 |
| Food | 9 | 6 | 3 |
| Res Mat | 25 | 26 | -1 |
| PE | 46 | 44 | 2 |
| IT | 22 | 22 | 0 |
| RE | 14 | 14 | 0 |
| Life | 20 | 20 | 0 |
| Science | 79 | 72 | 7 |
| English | 79 | 72 | 7 |
| Maths | 81 | 68 | 13 |
| **STAFF Available** | **611** | | |
| **Required** | | **562** | |
| **Difference** | | | **49** (47) |

**Figure 4.2** Issues identified and possible solutions.

## Figure 4.3 — Model known blocks including KS4 options

**128**

| | 1 | 2 | 3 | 4 | 5 | 6 | 7 | 8 | 9 | 10 | 11 | 12 | 13 | 14 | 15 | 16 | 17 | 18 | 19 | 20 | 21 | 22 | 23 | 24 | 25 |
|---|---|---|---|---|---|---|---|---|---|---|---|---|---|---|---|---|---|---|---|---|---|---|---|---|---|
| 7.1 | En | En | En | Ma | Ma | Ma | Sc | Sc | Sc | Re | Li | Ml | Ml | Ar | Gg | Gg | Hi | Hi | Dr | Pe | Pe | Rd | Mu | It | Te |
| 7.2 | En | En | En | Ma | Ma | Ma | Sc | Sc | Sc | Re | Li | Ml | Ml | Ar | Gg | Gg | Hi | Hi | Dr | It | Te | Pe | Pe | Rd | Mu |
| | | | | | | | | | | | | | | | | | | | | Rd | | It | | | |

| | 1 | 2 | 3 | 4 | 5 | 6 | 7 | 8 | 9 | 10 | 11 | 12 | 13 | 14 | 15 | 16 | 17 | 18 | 19 | 20 | 21 | 22 | 23 | 24 | 25 |
|---|---|---|---|---|---|---|---|---|---|---|---|---|---|---|---|---|---|---|---|---|---|---|---|---|---|
| 7.3 | En | En | En | Ma | Ma | Ma | Sc | Sc | Sc | Re | Li | Ml | Ml | Ar | Gg | Gg | Hi | Hi | Dr | Pe | Pe | Rd | Mu | It | Te |
| 7.4 | En | En | En | Ma | Ma | Ma | Sc | Sc | Sc | Re | Li | Ml | Ml | Ar | Gg | Gg | Hi | Hi | Dr | It | Te | Pe | Pe | Rd | Mu |
| | | | | | | | | | | | | | | | | | | | | Rd | | Mu | | | |

**111**

Options: **Opt 1** (cols 15–16) · **Opt 2** (cols 17–19) · **Opt 3** (cols 20–22) · **Opt 4** (cols 23–25)

| | 1 | 2 | 3 | 4 | 5 | 6 | 7 | 8 | 9 | 10 | 11 | 12 | 13 | 14 | Opt 1 | Opt 1 | Opt 2 | Opt 2 | Opt 2 | Opt 3 | Opt 3 | Opt 3 | Opt 4 | Opt 4 | Opt 4 |
|---|---|---|---|---|---|---|---|---|---|---|---|---|---|---|---|---|---|---|---|---|---|---|---|---|---|
| 11.1 | En | En | En | En | En | Ma | Ma | Ma | Sc | Sc | Sc | Sc | Pe | Li | St | St | Gg | Gg | Gg | TSc | TSc | TSc | Hi | Hi | Hi |
| 11.2 | En | En | En | En | En | Ma | Ma | Ma | Sc | Sc | Sc | Sc | Pe | Li | Bu | Bu | Ph | Ph | Ph | Ar | Ar | Ar | Rm | Rm | Rm |
| 11.3 | En | En | En | En | En | Ma | Ma | Ma | Sc | Sc | Sc | Sc | Pe | Li | Bu | Bu | Sp | Sp | Sp | Sp | Sp | Sp | Gg | Gg | Gg |
| 11.4 | En | En | En | En | | Ma | Ma | Ma | Sc | Sc | | Sc | Pe | Li | Mu | Mu | Ss | Ss | Ss | Fd | Fd | Fd | Dr | Dr | Dr |
| | | | | | | | | | | | | | | | Cz | Cz | Md | Md | Md | Hi | Hi | Hi | It | It | It |
| | | | | | | | | | | | | | | | Re | Re | Ss | Ss | Ss | | | | Gg | Gg | Gg |

**Figure 4.3** Model known blocks including KS4 options.

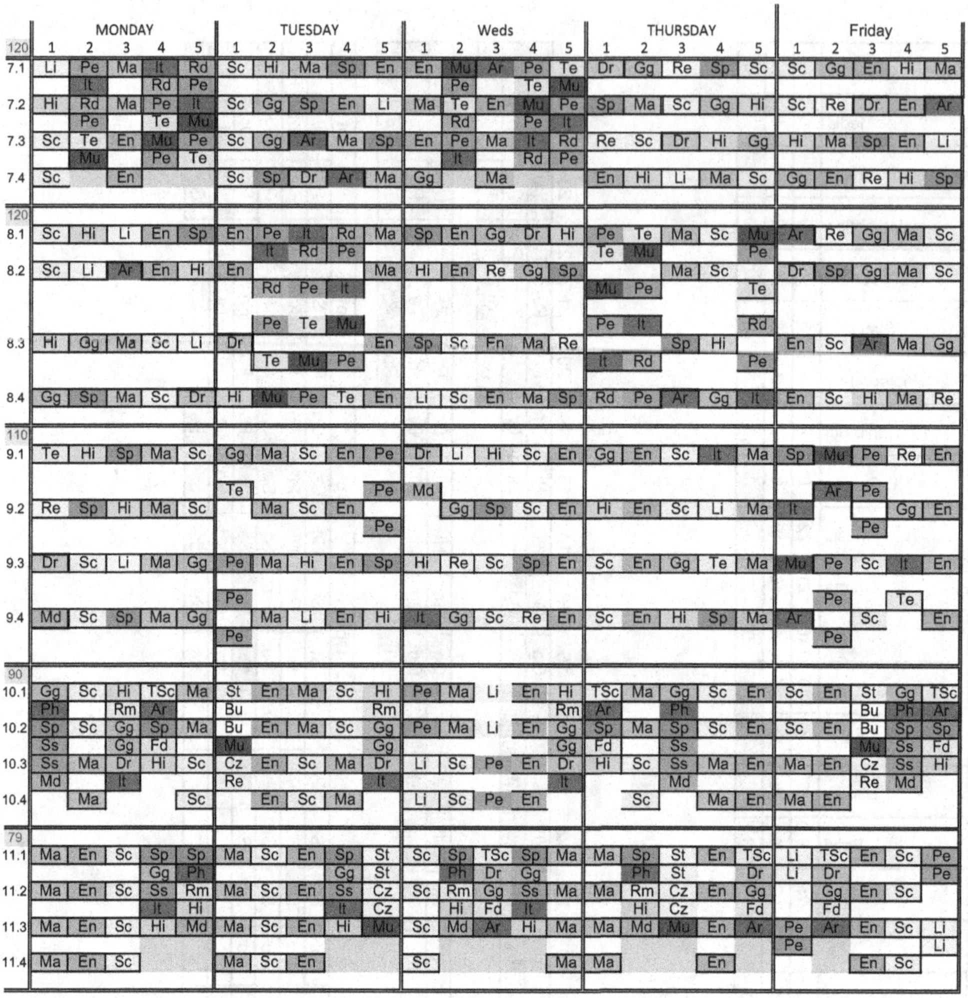

**Figure 4.4** Timetable core subjects for KS4 then KS3.

# Break and lunch time

When writing about managing break and lunch time, I'm going to take this as a "problem to be solved." If you don't have a problem with break and lunch time, if you release your pupils from lessons into the wider school community and they behave well and are kind to one another, eat responsibly and put rubbish in the bin, and turn up on time for the next lesson, that is wonderful news. Stick with whatever it is you're currently doing.

The main issues I've encountered at break and lunch time are pupils being unkind to one another, fights on the playground, silly behaviour such as water fights, pupils going to areas they are not permitted to go, pupils leaving rubbish or not picking it up when asked, and pupils being late to lessons after both breaks, and so the outlines below are intended to resolve one or more of these issues. Clearly, in your context, some of this may be relevant and some totally irrelevant, so feel free to use this as a prompt for thinking about your school.

We will go into duties later on in this chapter, but for now I'll say that the three keys to successful break and lunch time are great staff presence, appropriate length of break, and appropriate space management.

We've talked about the length of break earlier on in this chapter: the ideal length of break in the schools I've worked in is 25 minutes, and the ideal lunch is 35 minutes. In no school I've worked at did we have these length of breaks. I've found that lunch after 35 minutes often becomes challenging to manage, and 15- and 20-minute break times felt like pupils didn't quite have enough time to do everything they needed to do as well as line up ready for the next lesson. I'll state again: for morning break, have as long as you're able to give, up to 30 minutes; for lunch, have as short as you're able to give, ideally 35 to 40 minutes. I'll caveat this by saying I've worked almost my entire career in secondary schools; my understanding from primary colleagues is that morning break is almost always much shorter than 25 minutes – more like 10 to 15 minutes – and lunch time much longer, ranging from 45 minutes to an hour.

Before considering the space you will use, consider the staffing. In one school I worked at, lunch break was a full hour – a real challenge to staff but made much easier by having just four medium-size spaces where pupils could be. Each area had one member of staff manning it, and the "easiest" areas (the two small playgrounds, where there were fun games and the younger pupils tended to stay) could be staffed by lunchtime supervisors, with the support of SLT who did a circuit of all four areas multiple times over the hour. As SLT in that school, I'd spend the entire hour of lunch walking between the areas, and I rarely encountered any issues. I'll say as well that in that school the canteen was very large and the nearly 70% of free school meals pupils loved to use it, and if there had ever been issues before I joined the school, it could have been there, because the Headteacher herself staffed the canteen each and every day for the full hour, along with one or two more members of the SLT. It was a great lesson in hands-on leadership, and it made the Head incredibly visible for all pupils, the very vast majority of whom passed through the canteen each day. Having SLT and Heads be a visible presence is as important in primary as it is for secondary, particularly if your primary school breaks are staffed by non-teaching staff or midday meals supervisors who might not have the same relationships with all pupils as their trusted class teachers.

One easy way to improve break and lunch time experiences for pupils is to expand the variety and capacity of the activities on offer. Opening the library is fine, but unless you also have a selection of games for pupils to enjoy, it will quickly become another rowdy space. In my experience, children are remarkably good at knowing what they need to do in their "off" time to get their energy out – some will just want to sit at a picnic table and gossip; some will want to run around with a football. If your space doesn't allow for opening a football pitch, basketball hoops and table tennis tables can be a space-saving way to get ball games going for pupils who want this.

We'll go into duties below, but when considering break and lunch times, think carefully about how you will staff them. If your toilets are inside and you want pupils to be outside, think about what this will mean – will you allow pupils to move in and out of the building freely, for example? One school I worked at had pupils use the toilet only on their way out of the building, so the toilets needed to be staffed only at the start of the lunch break and teachers could then move back to have a break or move outside to continue their duty. One handy new-build school I visited had a block of toilets on the playground, making staffing much easier and the facilities more accessible. In general, I'd be concerned about allowing pupils total free movement of the building for their own safety – if you can't staff a space but a child is allowed there, it could become a space for harm.

As a member of the school's leadership team, assume you will be on duty every break and lunch time and don't be surprised about this. Breaks are for teachers too, but not for you – that's not the job you've chosen. Bear in mind you are likely to have significantly less contact hours than teachers, and although those free periods are anything but, they are time away from pupils to complete admin (which is what I observe 99% of teachers doing in their lunch breaks – I've yet to meet a teacher who gives themselves an actual break in the school day). In terms of managing yourself, I've always volunteered for canteen duty because I know if I don't eat I become really cranky, and this duty meant I was able to grab food at the same time as managing the pupils. Perhaps you need to leave the building – volunteer to man the playground in that case.

## Duties

I worked with a Deputy Head who used to say that doing a great duty was as important as teaching a great lesson, and in terms of pupil safety and wellbeing, I agree. It is worth investing time in duties and getting teachers to know how to do these well, rather than just publishing a rota and assuming they will comply.

Firstly, consider your duty points. They should be reasonable for one person to have eyes over an area, and not require staff to move to be able to see everything. Depending on teachers' loading and willingness, you might not be able to rely on teachers doing duties at lunchtime as well as breaktime. In the best schools I've worked in, teachers have understood they need to do both, but this is by no means a given. Other schools I've worked in have had to pay teachers to get the coverage needed at lunchtime. It is a critical investment if you need to do this. At the same time, teachers do need some down time – lunch time is not long, and they, like pupils, need to eat, use facilities, and set up for their next lesson. As a senior leader, try to always hold in your head how pressured teaching a full timetable is. I vividly remember how challenging my "duty day" always felt as a mainscale teacher.

In terms of manageable ways to staff duties, a "duty day" is not a bad idea. If teachers know that on Tuesdays they will have a very pressured day but the rest of the week they have all their breaks, that can be helpful. Having their duty day be on their lightest teaching day should be a given – no one should have six periods and three duties.

If teachers do multiple duties in a week, aim to ensure that they are always at the same point at the same time doing the same thing. It is much easier to manage – they will get very good at it, and they will be less likely to forget it. Particularly for teachers who don't teach in one classroom (in inner city schools, that is most teachers), the logistics of having to move from space to space are challenging enough without adding in varying duty points.

At the start of the year, have SLT run training on the different duty points. Do this for all points, because if a member of staff is ill, it will need to be covered – and try to timetable it in so that you seek cover for it in the same way as you would a lesson. I'd aim for only SLT to be asked to cover duties, but if teachers know what they're doing, many will (un)happily step into an empty duty spot. The number of times I've been the "duty checker" and seen unfamiliar faces who say something like "I noticed no one was here so I've stopped by" always astonishes me. Teachers, even the most over-worked, really do want the best for pupils.

And, finally, that role of duty checker is important – and if you're paying people, it becomes even more important, as we have a duty to the public purse to use funds appropriately. It's a good opportunity for SLT to be out visibly supporting as well as checking off each space. If a member of staff isn't on duty, follow up – kindly the first time and with genuine inquiry: is this time unmanageable for them? Use this as an opportunity to see if your duty points work: do you have full coverage? Are there any blind spots? Also see how staff are interacting with pupils. Is it working well and worth a "shout out" in staff briefing? Seeing staff playing with pupils as well as checking their area, and pupils happy and safe chatting away to a staff member who you can see is also visibly scanning to check all is well is great to see and worth celebrating. Or do people need a refresher? Is that a reminder in briefing, or a full session of duty practice in continuing professional development (CPD) time?

## Claire White, Trust Deputy Headteacher, Poltair School and Bodmin College (CELT), shares her approach to duties

*Duties. The very nature of the word sparks a reaction in people. For some, they embrace the notion of "a sense of duty" to "serve" others and simply get on with it, not really thinking twice about it. However, for most, it comes with the feeling of dread: the distraction from being prepared for the next lesson, the chance to get a drink and use the conveniences, a moment in time that could be better spent.*

*At my school, we believe that duties are an opportunity to model culture and to build important relationships. For this to be meaningful to staff, they must be intentionally scheduled and thoughtfully considered.*

*We believe that duties can have real impact in creating a positive culture, setting the tone for behaviour, strengthening relationships, and enabling children to enjoy school.*

*So, what have we done?*

1  *We keep the number of duties to a minimum with most staff doing a maximum of two break duties per week.*

2  *We eliminated before and after school duties for teachers – these can be busy times for teachers and can make the day feel stressful. Instead, pastoral staff and senior leaders do these, leaving teachers to focus on preparing for the day.*

3  *We try to place the duty adjacent to a non-contact period. It lessens the pressure on staff and means that it is easier for them to be punctual.*

4  *We identify specific duty areas and give guidance for how to do the duty successfully. We eliminate the "grey" by making expectations clear. This helps to ensure consistency across the week.*

5  *We have bells in the school day: 5 minutes before the day starts and 2 minutes before the end of both breaks. This signals the importance of moving promptly, and it takes the stress away of having to prompt, nag or sanction stragglers, reducing the stress for everyone.*

6  *We try to allocate staff to the areas that make the most sense. Our PE staff supervise sports areas for example, and we place form tutors, pastoral support staff and Heads of Year in areas where they will find their year groups. This encourages the building of relationships and means that we are playing to people's strengths.*

7  *We model positive interactions overtly. This means encouraging staff to talk to the children whilst on duty. We don't believe in having a "them and us" culture.*

8  *We buy duty coats for staff: in wet and windy weather nobody wants to be outside so we can at least make it bearable. Importantly, it helps the "team" ethos: staff feel part of what we are achieving together. Plus, it means that students can find an adult easily during a break time if needed. We also have duty radios. This helps staff to feel safe and makes follow up more convenient otherwise things get lost as people race off to teach or to a meeting.*

9  *Our Designated Safeguarding Lead and Behaviour Lead are always roaming at duty times. This visibility helps and encourages our students to interact with them but also allows for "hot spots" to be identified and for SLT to pivot and ensure that it is addressed quickly. It also means consistency is much easier to achieve.*

10  *We encourage our SLT to circulate at break times. This often means that there are often multiple staff in duty areas so we take the opportunity to send staff away so that they can have their break time back. Sometimes it's the little things that make the most difference to staff morale.*

Attention to detail matters in all forms of school leadership, as do reflection and a chance to test out that what you intended to do is what's happening. Duties shouldn't be any different: enabling children to enjoy their social times helps them to have the right head space for learning, but it doesn't need to be to the detriment to staff wellbeing. It's a delicate balance but one that can be achieved.

---

### Abby Hughes, Assistant Headteacher for Teaching and Learning at the West London Free School, explains how she manages duties

*Duties are not a very glamorous part of the school day. As you stand eating your lunch outside the KS4 toilets, one can begin to wonder whether a career in accountancy would really have been that bad. But what they lack in glamour, they make up for in utility: duties are absolutely essential for the smooth-running of the day, the creation of a safe and orderly atmosphere and the avoidance of unnecessary behaviour incidents.*

*Below are the things we do at the West London Free School (WLFS).*

1  *Decide your duty spots: What do pupils do before school, during break and lunch and after school in your setting? At WLFS, they are typically doing one of four things: queuing, eating, using the toilets or hanging out in their designated area. This is where staff are on duty. Duty locations are always under review; we add and remove as required.*

2  *Get an electronic copy of the school timetable on Excel: This allows you to filter by period to determine who is free ahead of changeovers, breaks, lunchtimes, end of the day, and so on. This makes assigning duties more straightforward, so, for example, the queue duty is assigned to someone who is free period 4 so they can be on their duty spot ahead of pupils arriving. With a split site like ours, we can also avoid assigning a duty to someone who would be coming back from the other site over break.*

3  *Create a magic spreadsheet: As I put a teacher's initials next to a duty, the number of duties each person has and how many minutes a week they are on duty is totted up in a separate tab. Magic. This allows me to ensure that staff are all assigned roughly the same time on duty each week, depending on their level of responsibility in the school.*

4  *Give a clear deadline: I ask for staff to look at the duty list on the first day of INSET (in- service training) and email me any changes by a chosen deadline. I am really clear about the importance of doing this – making changes is rarely just a straight swap and can have a knock-on effect. The duty rota needs to be enacted from the point at which pupils are on the site, so time is of the essence.*

5  *Monitor duties: We have a member of SLT on call at break and lunch. Their first job is check that all other staff members are on duty and to email staff members who haven't arrived. This year, we have also put all staff duties on their timetables on our management information system (MIS). This means that if a staff member is out of school, we are able to see that a duty is not going to be covered and make arrangements for this.*

6  *Create clear instructions: Each duty spot has a set of instructions that go with it. This should specify where staff member should stand to have the best view of the area – yes, Pastore's Perch is a thing even in the playground![1] It details the specific instructions for that area. For example, what precise time the bell should be rung or how pupils should stand when queueing. This year, we have invested in clip frames for each duty spot after seeing a post on social media from Astrea Academy Woodfields. These contain the instructions along with the rota for that spot, so it is easy to know who is missing and what to do for the member of staff covering it.*

7  *Reminders: There is so much going on in the first week of the school year and duties can be easily forgotten. For the first week, we send a reminder email at the start of the school day to all those who have a duty that day. We also ask staff to put their duties in their Outlook calendars with a reminder that pops up.*

8  *Provide training: We provide training to staff with particularly tricky duties such as running line-ups. For other duty spots, we encourage staff to use the same strategies that they would in the classroom when on duty (i.e. Pastore's Perch, Be Seen Looking etc.).[2] We talk about duties in briefings, shouting out staff who do an excellent job and reminding staff of the crucial role they play.*

My final tip is to be nice to whoever does your duty rota; it is a mammoth task!

## Wet break

Particularly if you are based in the UK, you will need to have a strong and tested plan for what to do at break time when it rains. There are clear operational concerns, and every school differs in space. I'll share here what has and has not worked in my experience of different schools.

What works well is a plan that is simple and clearly communicated to pupils. There will be optimal numbers of pupils in a single indoor space; one of the least successful wet break arrangements I experienced had three year groups in the sports hall with only two members of staff; the noise and chaos that emerged were quite something. I've also worked in schools where pupils are sent to form rooms at break, which is challenging to staff and leaves teachers exhausted and unprepared for their next lesson and can be a particular challenge for primary colleagues who are unlikely to have any respite due to their already-high contact time with their allocated class. At one school, we had large areas where pupils would be, but the rule was that the children had to be sitting down – somehow this had a magically calming effect, though as it was all-girls I can't tell if this would work in a mixed school as nicely.

Certainly, having all SLT on duty during wet break is a must. It is unfair to ask teachers to staff additional duties just because the heavens have happened to open.

Whatever the locations you send pupils to, ensure that you have clearly communicated:

- Where those locations are – ideally to pupils that morning in form time, having checked the forecast in the early morning

- To staff on duty outside where their new duty point should be – ensure that this is always the same change ("staff on playground duty, move to the canteen," for example)

- To staff and pupils that break time will be wet, so everyone knows at the time what to do – this is important. Do not rely on an email sent during lesson time – use a tannoy to announce it, or have staff visit classrooms the period before break to communicate this; or set up the pips to signal something everyone knows when they hear it ("Three long pips? Must be wet break today")

- With younger pupils, communicating what is and is not allowed at wet break is especially critical, particularly where they are using their classrooms during this time. Are they expected to be seated, or can they move about? What resources can they access, and what is the expectation for how these are packed away? These expectations may well vary by age group, so ensure that there is clarity amongst middle and senior leaders and that this is communicated with pupils.

Of course, another method is to ignore wet break completely and just ensure that pupils are equipped with umbrellas and waterproof coats. This might not win you fans from parents and soaking staff members, but it is one way of going about it – after all, it is rare to have torrential downpours, and most of us are used to leaving the house when it rains as adults – it is hardly that we need to avoid the outdoors totally 200 days a year.

## The canteen

While your school's duty points will differ, practically all secondary schools have a canteen. In my experience, this has been one of the most critical areas of school life to manage. Again, primary colleagues will find much of this section very different: in small primaries, pupils eat lunch in classrooms due to a lack of large shared space, and where pupils eat altogether in a canteen, the number of children involved can render this a less challenging space to staff – although some of the advice below may well be helpful to primary leaders, particularly those in larger settings.

To begin with, assuming most children will use the canteen, it is important to have a system that means they can eat quickly and peacefully as well as where they are encouraged to be tidy and clean up after themselves. As with all routines outlined in the first chapter, I'd urge children to be explicitly taught these expectations, and I might use signs around the canteen to remind them of these expectations.

I've worked in schools that use a range of ways to get children through lunch, from the highly controlled and orchestrated family lunch through to free seating. While family lunch has been my personal favourite, it is not everyone's, and it takes a vast amount of staffing to get it right each day, not to mention the machinations of ensuring that every child pays for it. (I recently saw an advertisement for a local secondary school that boasted that *all* children were given free school meals there regardless of parental income – not something I'd realised schools could do. If you want to run family lunch, I'd budget it accordingly, and if you can afford to simply subsidise the lot, it would make a lot of sense to do that operationally – otherwise, you will be using extortionate amounts of administrative time collecting debts and chasing payments.)

Free reign in the canteen has never been my favourite, and in a range of schools I've found these canteens to be noisier and a source of more mischief as well as harder to clean (because the children have made more mess and it hasn't been noticed), though I have no doubt they're the right thing in some schools. Indeed, given all the many things leaders need to think about when running a school, you may ask yourself if canteen seating is one of them.

Finally, you could run a hybrid, perhaps one of fixed seating – either where everyone has an assigned space, which a lot of schools ran during the pandemic, or where year groups are assigned to a particular area. This can make issues easier to follow up on and can be good for urging form tutors and Heads of Year to check in with their children. I've also worked with a "fill the next seat" system, which tends to result in children not sitting with their closest friends (though some will queue together, surprisingly few work out how to queue with a very large group of friends). This means children have the potential of making new friends over lunch as well as no clusters of large groups and so a calmer, quieter experience overall.

The more staff in your canteen, the better. I've previously worked in schools that did something as simple as giving staff who sat with pupils a free lunch. This needs to be clearly explained, as I've seen a handful of staff take advantage of this and not engage with pupils at all while sitting and eating their free lunch at a pupil-designated table. But rewarding staff for engaging with pupils over lunch feels like a quick win: it's important for teachers to eat during the school day, there is food available, and the more adults chatting to pupils you have in a canteen, the calmer and more controlled the experience is for everyone.

Having a system for children and staff to pay for lunch is a necessity that isn't often written about, probably like a lot of things this chapter will touch on. Most primaries will operate a pre-pay system for lunches rather than use checkouts, and at secondary level, I've yet to work in a school with a cash checkout; I suspect these will become more and more rare as the years go on. Most schools I've worked at use a fingerprint to link to a Parent Pay account, which parents add money to and which is then deducted at the till. This prevents any pupils from bullying other pupils into handing over a lunch card, for example – they simply can't force another pupil to pay for their lunch.

No system is fool-proof, and inevitably pupils will not always know how much money is on their account, leading to some awkward conversations at the till. It is worth remembering this and ensuring your tills are managed appropriately. It is challenging, in my experience, for teachers to man tills for this reason: they know the pupils and find it very hard to tell them they don't have enough money for lunch. I've worked in schools where Heads of Year (HoYs) oversee this, and the teachers on the tills send pupils to the HoY, who makes contact with parents. This rapidly became untenable for the heartbreaking reason that too many parents were not adding money to their child's account.

Depending on your school's intake, you might decide, as many schools I've worked in have, to give a free sandwich or similar to these pupils. At the same time, having a pastoral member of staff involved is key: one pupil claimed a free sandwich for two weeks, saying their parents could not afford lunch – however, it transpired her brother in a different year group had no problem paying for lunch. When the parents were contacted, the HoY found out the girl had been given money to top up her account, but it wasn't quite making it to school each day.

I've no doubt this is extremely rare, and you might want to set aside some budget to cover meals for those who cannot pay, and you may not choose to put your strongest pastoral team near tills at lunchtime – most likely they are more impactful elsewhere.

I'd always advise SLT to eat school meals as often as possible, particularly in schools with high numbers of pupils on free school meals. At least someone on SLT needs to eat in the canteen each day and check firsthand that the food is plentiful enough and good enough for that to be your main meal of the day, as that will be the case for some pupils. There is a balance here: the food needs to be tasty, though we can't judge that by home standards: cooking at scale and with the statutory limits on salt intake, for example, set by government regulations for good reason, mean you're never going to have a restaurant or even home-cooked meal standard – but it should be tasty and edible. Having something healthy is also critical: you need to raise flags if the food is too unhealthy, as again this will not work for children for whom this is their main source of nutrition. At the same time, in my experience, vegetables and the like are better being hidden in meals. Offering a lush side salad is something you will find canteen staff throwing away in bulk at the end of lunchtime. Look at the dessert on offer: cake is fine once a week, but ideally dessert should be on the healthier side as often as possible – again, I've seen too many pupils eat solely dessert, including those on free school meals.

Go down the rows and look at what children aren't eating. This is how I noticed poor-quality meat, for example – it is rare to find children not eating meat, so if they leave it, ask why – and if large numbers leave it, it is an automatic flag for your kitchen staff.

A classic issue I've found with kitchen managers is many feel they should be updating menus continually, to provide interest in the food. In my experience, children are far more likely to enjoy habit than variety. A two-week menu provides more than enough variety and enables kitchen staff to get really good at these ten meals. Finding ten nutritious, healthy meals that the children enjoy and eat most of is extremely challenging and a great thing to do. In my opinion, this outweighs the experiments with different dishes children will tend to avoid. Helping kitchen managers and chefs to understand this is critical. That is different, of course, to celebrating specific days – for example, they may wish to offer Chinese food on Chinese New Year. I'd advise chefs to offer this as one additional dish rather than replacing the offer – and when you do this, you will be surprised how few opt for novelty over what they know and like.

Finally, if you're responsible for kitchen and canteen staff, remember the importance of their training and development. As they are pupil-facing, they will need the same safeguarding induction and top-up training as all staff; they are unlikely to work the same hours, so think through when and how this will be shared. Sending your school chef to visit other school kitchens on inset days to get ideas for strong menus or efficient kitchen practices will be helpful, and giving enough notice for this so they can organise for their remaining team to prep any inset food required for teachers will be important.

## External assessments

There are some aspects of school life you will want to be good at and some you *need* to be good at. Exams and external assessments are in the latter category. The scope and scale of regulations surrounding external assessment are greater than leaders assume before taking on responsibility for this post, and it is critical for pupils that this aspect of school life be well managed, because, of course, exams lead to life choices for them.

One Executive Principal had me read the Joint Council for Qualifications (JCQ) "Instructions for Conducting Exams" ("ICE") guidance each September – a very good idea. For primary colleagues, the Department for Education's assessment and reporting arrangements ("ARA") is the key document here. More challenging than mere reading of the regulations is to map where each of these occurs in your own exams policy and your Exam Officer's plan for the year. I'd recommend reading the guidance alongside both and ensuring that your own school's policy and operational planning are reflecting the rules and regulations meticulously.

For secondary colleagues, having a subscription to "Exams Office" (www.theex amsoffice.org) for yourself, your Headteacher, and your Exams Officer is critical.

I'm sure other bodies offer this, but I can vouch for their "get ready for exams" checklists and the training and support on offer. Using the checklists to work with your Exams Officer is an easy way of ensuring that your centre is compliant with the guidance, and having your Exams Officer do their training is essential development and support for their role. Indeed, I would go so far as to suggest that you also do this training so you know intimately the demands and expectations of the role.

Make the time to meet with your Exams Officer weekly. For an experienced Exams Officer, they might be used to being left alone and find this unsettling; however, many I've worked with feel this is quite a lonely role and will welcome the interaction this will provide. You will need to support them to recruit and train invigilators – a massive responsibility and critical piece of operational work – as well as to ensure the logistics of the exam hall work for the wider school community and the regulations. They will need, before the exam period, to have meetings with the site team and a strong and trusting relationship to allow them to meet the guidance in the set-up of the hall.

Exams Officers are unique among school support staff in that not only do they need to work with a wide variety of staff across the school, they also often need to give instructions and directions to middle and senior leaders in the school. This is usually while receiving modest pay. If you manage an Exams Officer, work to support them with this. For example, when Heads of Department (HoDs) need to confirm exam entries, be proactive in helping the Exams Officer with these interactions – either coaching them for a challenging "chasing" conversation or simply offering to be copied into the email – to which you can add your own "this is really critical and I can support you with cover if you need time to get this done" to the email thread.

The role of Exams Officer is challenging and demanding; it is also a very lonely role in a school. While multi-academy trusts (MATs) might have networks established for Exams Officers in different schools to collaborate and ask questions, this is by no means assured. Support the Exams Officer in making connections with local schools so they have someone knowledgeable and, hopefully, experienced to turn to for a second opinion in any thorny matters.

## In-school exams

Again, primary colleagues are largely exempt from this section: the focus for most primary colleagues is on external assessments feeling as familiar and unthreatening as possible, and given their confinement to small numbers of pupils (relative to secondary colleagues), these are often managed largely by class teachers and within usual class spaces.

In secondary schools and larger primaries in the upper key stages, organising in-school formal assessments might be a role for a member of SLT. This is in effect like a miniature version of what the Exams Officer does for external exams, only with far more pupils and far fewer regulatory restrictions.

You will first need to work with HoDs to ascertain the requirements for the papers they would like pupils to sit: how many papers, how long each paper is, and any special requirements for sitting it. For example, the Art department will most likely not require an exam room but probably will want pupils in a subject-specific room with access to Art materials.

After you've got all the requirements for each year group, you will need to check this is sound. If the English department want every year group to sit two two-hour exams, not only will that be an enormous amount of time for pupils, it will also create a marking load for their teachers and a burden of feedback it might be challenging to deliver. It is worth deciding the parameters of your exam schedule prior to talking to HoDs, so you can pre-empt their enthusiasm for exams and say: "We are only going to have a seven-day window, so every subject will have one one-and-a-half-hour paper at Key Stage 3, unless you have a very good reason for more papers or fewer." Or whatever your parameters are! Ultimately, as discussed in Chapter 2, it is incredibly difficult to create in-school assessments which produce valid and reliable detail, and with this in mind, spending a huge amount of teacher and leader time on these might not be the best use of pupils' learning time.

The other operational consideration is rooming. While you may aspire to have every pupil in an exam hall, this is unlikely to work unless you are blessed with so much space you're able to do this without significant disruption. Given that pupils are unlikely to have had an assembly hall or sports hall for the duration of GCSEs in many schools, consider carefully the impact on whole-school experience for pupils to continue to use these spaces for in-school exams. Many leaders will prioritise one or two year groups to have the "proper exam experience." Of course, you may feel that this is a priority and that in the sunniest weeks of the year having the sports hall out of action is not a problem for PE lessons. This is far less of a concern for primary leaders, who will tend to staff exams in pupil rooms – including more formal tests like SATs (standardised assessment tests).

If pupils are sitting exams in classrooms, this does add more of an invigilation burden on teachers. They will be tempted to sit down and get on with marking, as who wouldn't? So be explicit with your instructions to them of how you expect teachers to work during exam weeks to ensure that pupils are being vigilantly watched, so you can be assured that the work they write is genuinely their own. You will want to have SLT deployed to enforce exam conditions and to support teachers with sending out anyone who speaks or tries to communicate for a strong conversation about what happens if you do that in a real exam.

In-school exams inevitably require a great deal of staff time, and so it makes sense to pause meetings, professional development, and any new initiatives for the exam and marking period. This is another reason why schools should think very carefully about how many in-school exam periods they wish to hold in one academic year.

Ensure that your communication with staff is clear and reiterated: it is worth having a professional development session on running exams as well as one set aside for departments to moderate work together. You might want to reiterate key messages in briefings and a short email to stamp the central messages and ensure they land. At one school I worked at with complex exam arrangements, an email was sent during the period each day with staff names and classes who were in different spaces. Although I rarely advocate clogging inboxes, in this instance the overwhelming feedback was that teachers found this a helpful reminder of complex logistics as well as supporting them to answer queries from their classes or tutor groups about the day's arrangements.

Supporting tutors to communicate with their tutees will be critical in this period. Sending a single slide or having a clear exam timetable tutors can run through each day with their classes will be helpful as well as any assemblies or messages focusing on revision and exam techniques so children are fully confident in what they are meant to be doing to make the most of these sessions.

The length of time you give staff to mark should be reasonable without being exceptionally lengthy. It can be longer if you have fewer exam periods strangely – pupils seem more content to wait for results when it rarely happens, but frequent marks almost fuels their appetite to know more, sooner. I've heard leaders positioning the marking period over half terms or holidays "so staff have more time to mark." I would strongly advise against this. The holidays in teaching, though plentiful, are regarded by most teachers as necessary to recover and be their best selves for the term ahead. More sensible might be to advocate for whole-class feedback and tick-and-flick approaches to exam marking, especially if the marking load is high and the delay for returning papers will be lengthy – detailed comments written on work done three weeks ago are unlikely to help anyone.

Feedback on exams is essential, and we've touched on this in Chapter 2. I drew there on an example of a colleague who marked his science papers onto an Excel sheet but didn't write marks on exam papers. That meant pupils were listening carefully to the feedback when they got their papers back and weren't distracted by their overall mark and corresponding grade, which was revealed only at the end of the feedback lesson.

Overall, in-school assessments can serve many purposes. Be clear about what those purposes are for your context. In the schools I've worked at, they have been most useful to prompt revisiting and therefore engaging prior learning of core concepts that will come up again over the years, to foster habits of focus in revision and during exams, and to get pupils used to the place they will eventually sit nationally standardised exams. Do not rely on these periods to drive learning for the whole year – the most important thing is the learning that pupils do every day in every lesson, not the preparations they undertake for a short exam period.

## Reporting to parents

For secondary colleagues, following on from in-school exams come parent reports; for primary colleagues, these might come earlier in the year to enable pupils to

action feedback before the end of the academic year. While it is a reasonable expectation that families are told how children are getting on in school annually, over
the years these have come to be much slimmer and more data-driven, including
for primary colleagues who might now give a "grade" for effort and attainment
rather than an overly wordy written report. While teacher workload is undoubtedly improved by not writing individualised comments for every child they teach,
this does mean we must be mindful that parents are receiving a lot of quantitative
data, which isn't always easy to understand.

Accessibility for parents is key. I've worked in schools that use colour coding
with pupil results, but this inevitably leads to simplifications. It's a balance and
knowing your parent community is important. We were once more concerned with
pupil progress to target grades, and this can easily be RAG-ed (red: not progressing
to target; amber: on track to target; green: above target), although there is now some
reasonable concern that target grades may be, themselves, limiting for pupils and
teachers. Also, for pupils with very low starting points, seeing a sea of green could
send the message they're ready to sweep 9s at GCSE, but this could be very misleading. Target grades might cap potential.

It is tempting to use a percentage to show how well pupils have done, and certainly that is what the school I went to used, and I've worked in one other school
which shared percentages. These are clear and easy for anyone to understand; a
concern is that some subjects grade more harshly than others, or some exams can
be easier; a 62% in one subject might be fantastic, and 82% in another might be
disappointing. Having teachers convert these to grades could support parents to
understand how good or not good the percentage is – they could allocate the top
10% of marks to a grade A, for example. It might help to show both the percentage
and the converted mark; if there is a large spread of results, this might make it more
confusing. You will really need to mock up your report options and run it by some
helpful colleagues for their thoughts. Having a clear and simple rationale written
prior to the raw marks will help.

Using the GCSE numbers has pros and cons as well: on the pro side, parents
should be familiar with the grading system for national exams. On the other hand,
using the GCSE numbers could lend your internal data a false sense of validity
and reliability you just cannot guarantee in an in-school assessment. Parents might
therefore be well within their rights to be angry at you for misleading them when
their progeny, getting 7s throughout KS3, suddenly get 5s in the real thing.

Another way some schools support parents to understand the progress of their
child is to give the child's percentage next to the class average, or the year group
average, for that test. Excluding outliers (e.g. remove from this the child who scores
0% because they were caught cheating so achieved no marks) will be important in
making this meaningful. Again, this runs the risk of leading to despair or compla-
cency for pupils. With some pupils, sharing the top percentage scored will drive
them to do better; again, others will find this dispiriting. (Imagine achieving 43%
and the top score was 97%; it might feel deflating and like an impossible gap to

scale.) If you like the idea of this, run the numbers and pull a random report and just put yourself in the shoes of the pupil receiving it. Will it make them feel like they can work hard and do better? Then think about the parents. Will they understand how well or not well their child is doing?

The most important thing we can do in the report to parents is tell them what they can do to help their children do well in that subject. Of course, we could give generic advice, but parents are going to be able to take in only so much information. Use this as an opportunity to tell parents the things their children need support in. Your HoDs might draft three bullet points of parent actions, and these are likely to be the same for almost all children. Making these simple, accessible, and easy to do is critical – most parents long for more guidance on how to help their child be successful.

Data-based reports are complex, and what we gain in time efficiency and a veneer of objectivity from a lot of numbers on a page, we lose in nuance about the particular child. It almost makes me want to say that perhaps once a year we should be writing two or three individualised sentences about each child we teach. Though for teachers who see 20 classes a week at KS3, clearly this is not a good use of their time, if it is even feasible off the back of the marking of 600 pupils' exams.

## School governance

A strong set of school governors can add real value to school improvement, but there are many horror stories of unsupportive or uninformed governors. An uninformed governing body is a real liability: you will need to work well with your governors or it will impact your leadership and management grading when Ofsted (Office for Standards in Education, Children's Services and Skills) arrive.

For academies, the legal governance aspects tend to be held at Trust level by education experts –regional directors or heads of education for the Trust. The governing body is then a Local Governing Body, intended to advise and question but without the additional role of being able, for example, to let Headteachers go and appoint the next one. Clearly, a governing body with such powers is even more critical to your school's success, and it is worth investing time in recruiting the right people.

You will want some kind of application and light touch interview process to secure great governors. Governors can add real value in areas not normally covered by teaching expertise, such as finance, marketing, and legal. Parent governors or governors from the local community can provide a vital insight into your school community and reflect parent voice in a way that supports ensuring that your school is meeting the needs of the community. It is worth being explicit during the application and interview process that it will be critical that governors take a whole-school view and avoid being overly influenced by their own child's experience: they cannot use this position to beat the drum for the specific concerns of a single child, however tempting and natural that may be for a parent. Digging into this with a scenario ("How would you react if your child received a suspension you felt was unfair?") might support this: see to what extent they would envisage using their governance role in difficult situations.

Whether your governing body is local or not, having a fortnightly call with the Chair of Governors is important to keep them in the loop of the day to day of what is happening in school. This need not be lengthy but will just ensure that they are better able to plan and run meetings with up-to-date knowledge of what is going on. Similarly, if members of SLT have responsibility that maps to your governors, have them organise regular touch points – perhaps a school visit once a half term or a quick call – for example, your safeguarding Vice Principal might meet with your safeguarding link governor; your community governor might meet with the member of SLT who is working on improving links with parents.

In terms of Governing Body meetings, the key is for these to be open and honest: governors must know the reality of your school. It is also worth being explicit and clear about workload – of teachers and leaders – so governors are less likely to suggest or push for things that don't make sense at the current time. There is plenty of guidance available from government that governors might acquaint themselves with and you might signpost them to should they ask for things that aren't reasonable – like weekly trips for pupils or data packs that go far beyond data you currently collect.

As the school governor role is a voluntary one, having them spend time in school regularly may be a challenge. Nonetheless, it is worth calendaring at least some of your meetings during the school day, so governors have an opportunity to spend time in school either before or after the meeting.

## Office administration

A well-organised office can make life easier for teachers, pupils, and parents. So much of a well-functioning school relies on its administrative function. It is also increasingly challenging to recruit excellent members of staff to this area of school life, with a cost-of-living crisis driving many professionals out of this space – traditionally underpaid and occasionally undervalued. Ensuring that the office space is well managed is one way to retain great people. Ensuring flexibility can also support retention by, for example, having staggered shifts so staff can manage childcare commitments.

When recruiting to the administrative team, it is equally as important they like children and communicate well with them as you'd expect from teaching professionals. Administrative colleagues need to be a mix of polite, kind, and firm – more challenging than it sounds. Overly firm and pupils and parents might feel unwelcome; overly indulgent and pupils will find excuses to visit reception during lessons.

Any school office is a fast-paced, rapidly changing environment – quite different from non-school offices I have experience of. It is therefore critical that office staff are not easily stressed.

The functions of the school office will vary but will often include management of absences, letters such as permission slips, managing the parent payment system and administration of free school meals, updating school display and the school website, and holding pupil records. In the best-run schools I know of, the office has also held photocopying for the whole staff body – a significant role, normally held in isolation by a single member of staff.

Whatever the functions your office takes on, ensure that colleagues have clarity on their role and the particular responsibilities that lie within it, and check by asking them that this is a reasonable expectation. Be curious as to how office time is spent – sometimes there are efficiencies that could support workload, or jobs being done that are duplicated elsewhere in the school staff body.

Ensuring that reception is safe is critical by, for example, having a buzzer with a video and doors that must be opened by reception staff – or at least a second set of doors leading onto the school that are locked unless a staff member opens them, usually with a fob.

Ensure that your administrative team receive training and development just as will be the case with all staff members. Particularly important will be safeguarding training and training on managing parents. The parents who find themselves in reception, particularly those without appointments, do not typically tend to be the school's least challenging, so ensuring that reception staff have training and the support of a quickly responsive SLT will be critical. If SLT meets after school on any particular day, ensure that a more senior middle leader is assigned to support the reception area during that meeting time so colleagues feel supported by the teaching staff.

## Attendance monitoring

A particularly critical role in the administrative team is the individual who records absences. I recall vividly the first time I overheard the absence manager at one school speaking with a parent. It was firm but kind: "A headache? Have you given her paracetamol? Is she feeling any better? Great, so you can send her in now and we'll keep an eye." She was so assured and confident in what she was saying but without being dismissive of the pupil's pain.

While, in primary settings, a member of the administrative team normally holds absence management alongside a host of other responsibilities, this area is usually a full-time role for a secondary colleague. Ensuring that this individual has a supportive senior leader as their line manager who can involve them in the right meetings and support them to do their best work is important. The role has a large administrative function, working with registers, letters, and student files; it is also one requiring regular contact with colleagues. For example, if this individual is chasing people to complete registers, this can be a frustrating aspect to the role. As SLT, you will need to add your clout to support them in some cases, either by being copied into emails or through determining a whole staff training or briefing is required. In primary schools, the Headteacher or at least the Vice Principal should touch base with their administrative team frequently on reasons for absence and suggested actions.

While this individual may be able to undertake parent meetings – and I've worked with some superb colleagues who were happy and able to do this – it may require training and support to begin with to ensure that meetings have the tone and the content you would expect.

## Line management

No matter what your role, you will need to meet colleagues for line management. The frequency of this meeting will be determined by your school's policy, though I'd always advocate for shorter, more frequent meetings where possible. For example, if the policy is fortnightly meetings of a full period, you might instead meet for 25 minutes each week. That said, ensuring that you stick to time is important. Being on time for line management and never going over time are two important aspects of time keeping: if you have an emergency occur once, that is one thing; if you are regularly late, it might not be the right time for you. Show colleagues you respect their time.

Trying to keep line management about the "big stuff" can be a real challenge. In *Culture Rules*, I advocate a few things: plan the meeting (time is precious – prepare for it and use it well), ask them what they want to cover first (so they don't spend the first part of the meeting waiting to speak), schedule time to talk about the stuff that really matters (their professional development, for example), and ask them for feedback. (I have a whole chapter on this in *Culture Rules*.)

Line management is some of the best professional development there is, so it is a huge responsibility to do this well with your people. Through your meetings, you will (hopefully) quickly ascertain whether the individual requires more stretch or more support, and this is a key time you can use to do either.

---

### Tom Turnham, Headteacher at Lyndhurst Primary School, Camberwell, London, outlines his approach to working with middle leaders

*When I think of middle leaders, I always think of unbridled energy and enthusiasm… And then I remember that in my time as a middle leader that enthusiasm was often directed in the wrong way, leading me to feel frustrated. The most important thing to do as a leader is to be really clear on parameters. By this I mean being really clear on what your middle leaders are responsible for and can make unilateral decisions on, and what they need to run by someone else first. It sounds so obvious yet is so often overlooked.*

*It's worth also considering how you want middle leaders to communicate both with staff and you. I prefer centralised messages rather than lots of disparate emails, so I ask that middle leaders feed in their communications requests to the senior team to send in the weekly bulletin.*

*I'm clear with middle leaders that we may ask them to pause on some changes as the staff as a body can only manage so many changes at a time. To manage this, I ask them to keep up to date action plans which I review and discuss with them termly. In this way, I can see overlap between areas of responsibility and tackle change more efficiently. I am a big believer in lean processes, so I ask middle leaders to keep all monitoring and budgeting on their action plan so that it is a one-stop-shop for their area. This means that they have only one concise document to deal with and I can see in a snapshot their direction of travel. When I feedback, I tend to do it in writing and frame it as a series of questions that allow them to review their plan, and I always offer the chance to meet to discuss the points. I find that sending this feedback in writing stops a leader feeling defensive, and the use of questions helps support the idea that we are working together. I always start the feedback with positives and successes that I have noticed either in the document or in their leadership—it goes without saying that these have to be authentic.*

*As Headteacher, I meet formally with middle leaders half termly. During this time, I update them on issues like budgets that will impact and inform their decision making, and discuss the priorities that have come up for the school as a whole. I create release time with middle leaders regularly and ensure that for some of those sessions a senior leader is with them to model good monitoring and to have discussions, as being a middle leader can be lonely – you can easily lose perspective or fall into common traps. This also allows middle leaders to feel that they are supported, it allows for solution focussed discussion rather than judgement. I spend a lot of time asking if issues are general or individual-specific, as I find that supports middle leaders to formulate a plan of action to fix them. I also model this in the way that I deal with difficult conversations or managing change.*

*I remember fondly being a middle leader and looking for every step I could take to excel, and so I focus on that when thinking about my middle leaders: I ask about their ambitions and suggest things that they should get under their belt. The national professional qualifications (NPQs) have been great to develop leaders, but again these need to be framed around a conversation about development and not just given out thoughtlessly.*

*Remember being a middle leader is a learning curve—give them opportunities to sit in and observe, to interview, to be involved in discussions about finance. Let them learn about leadership, and if you have middle leaders who aren't aligned to your way of working, spend time explaining your strategy and vision. Discuss why buy-in is important and highlight the importance of middle leaders playing their part in public and bringing their concerns to you in private—and mean that: engage in genuine conversation when they have concerns. After all, you might find that they are right and you are wrong!*

# Budgets

Although you are unlikely to have direct responsibility for budgets until Headship, it is worth asking the Head for the budget for your area and tracking it. This can support you to make better decisions in your area and prepare you for your next steps if you are interested in pursuing Headship.

Managing school budgets is often, at a MAT level, largely done by financial professionals. They calculate the school's income, which is based on per-pupil funding and any additional funding streams (free schools meals, for example; this does change rather frequently but, in the past, has included things like government top-ups for pension funds and national grants). If your school population is fluctuating, then, of course, so will your budget. Then the budget is laid out, normally in staff and non-staff costs.

The greatest aspect of any budget is the staff cost, and this goes up each year for individual members of staff with pay increments or pay awards or both. Ensuring that you have a strong calculation to determine how many teachers you require in each department is therefore critical. There is currently excellent advice and guidance on how to budget for curriculum-led financial planning on the Department for Education's website.[3]

Connected to budgets, even if you are part of a MAT, you may still need to determine additional payments, or Teaching and Learning Responsibility (TLR) payments. Though benchmarks are set in the national pay award, it may be your responsibility to determine which level is most appropriate for individuals. TLR 1 is the largest amount, normally reserved for extensive middle leadership positions like core HoDs or Heads of Year. TLR 3 is the smallest, normally for small, one-off, and time-limited projects. TLR 2 is still substantial at the top end and might be used for Heads of smaller Departments. Ensuring that you have thought through the rationale for these is critical: if you are paying some HoDs more, you need to be able to state why: Do they manage a large team? Do they deliver multiple qualifications over different key stages? Staff will rarely dig into what one another are being paid, but each time you advertise for a new TLR, bear in mind that some staff will be measuring that advertisement against their current role and thinking whether their current pay is fair.

When I reorganised TLR amounts, there were some heads of very small departments who were paid much larger amounts than was in reality fair or sustainable and there were others with more extensive responsibilities who were paid less. If your budget allows, it is best to raise the pay of those you identify as being underpaid but not to cut pay of others – instead, wait for them to be promoted or to leave, then readvertise the role at its true level. If this isn't possible, you will need to weigh up whether it is worth having the conversation to decrease salary in the interests of a fair or balanced budget. In general, these conversations are tough, and even when they are done by the most adept manager, you run the risk of losing the member of staff or at least of their feeling devalued and deflated. Think carefully about whether such a conversation is essential.

Your non-staff budget should include money set aside for expensive projects, such as maintaining the school's grounds and equipment (like information technology). You also have to make the call about spending the entire annual budget or leaving some of it in reserves. There isn't one right answer, and it generally depends how financially prudent you prefer to be, but I'd hazard that it's probably a good idea to have something in reserves – which is easier said than done in the current financial climate.

If you have a member of staff managing your budget, make time to meet with them weekly. In my experience, this need not take longer than 15 or 20 minutes most weeks. This is where you can check your current budget and see whether you can make room for any particular recruits or projects you are keen to run. Even if you're not planning recruitment, you will need to update this person on any new recruits or resignations so they can plan accordingly. It is also worth going through line by line a couple of times a year and sense-checking things like department budgets against actual spend, as this can help to identify savings and to identify areas where departments genuinely do require a higher budget for future years. It will also be where your finance team can flag any overspend ("It's only February, but you have spent 80% of the photocopying budget"), and you can decide what to move money from and to.

Moving a school from deficit to surplus is a challenge that many new leaders come across. By not spending on new staffing positions or new projects and by double-checking that no department is overstaffed or that you have the right number of support staff, this can be done quickly in schools with high turnover: very often, there are more staff than needed through legacy staffing arrangements, and even one member of staff leaving and not being replaced will make a tremendous difference to budgets.

Budgets are the aspect of leadership many fear, usually through lack of familiarity, but it is worth spending the time to understand every line of the budget once. It is surprising how doing this will allow most educational leaders to spot discrepancies or strange assumptions which can easily be corrected.

## Working with Unions

Unions are an important part of our education system. The work done at a national level has immense importance at a school level, particularly in setting salaries and defining conditions. School leaders should carefully consider their in-school representatives and how best to work with them. Some leaders take the attitude not to consult union representatives, which is a shame. Although some representatives will misrepresent their own interests as those of members, I've found, in general, that most are very clued into how many teaching staff are feeling.

Therefore, I'd advocate having a lunch together once every half term to discuss their concerns. Making it lunch makes it feel less formal, so you or they may prefer a timetabled meeting. (And if they are giving up their lunch, ensure that it is something delicious and feels like a treat – I only suggest lunch as finding time with multiple members of staff who are often your fully loaded teachers can be a challenge.) Over the course of your meeting, ask for any member concerns and try to ascertain the scale by simply asking: "How many people feel this? One? One to five? More than five?" This will usually remove any pet peeves from your list of considerations.

You should also ask union representatives for any ideas that are coming to them – I've heard some fantastic gems in my meetings with union representatives that genuinely work to improve the school. Of course, you will want to up the number of meetings during any national negotiations. Remaining neutral is important, particularly if you are part of a MAT where the work with unions might also be conducted at a national level.

I've worked with local union representatives in only one borough, so I have no way of telling if this is usual, but I've found them to be eminently sensible. Having your joint meetings with in-school and local representatives is a good way of keeping the local unions informed of the school's current work and current challenges. Building those relationships of mutual trust and respect will be harder in some areas and contexts than others, but starting from an understanding that everyone in the room deeply cares about the pupils as well as the pay and conditions of school staff does no harm.

## Meetings

I hate meetings. Or, rather, I hate almost all meetings. But that's probably because I don't run them well enough. In a well-run meeting, I come out feeling excited about the future and clear about my next steps. I'm sure many people have felt otherwise when coming out of meetings with me! Having this on your mind as the driving force behind your meetings can help: how do I want people to feel after this meeting?

Meetings in school range from short, informal, or ad hoc meetings to the set piece that is an SLT meeting. For informal meetings without an agenda, I'd just stay actions-focused and note actions decided to follow up more formally to save great ideas and intentions being lost. For any more formal meetings, make the distinction between items which are information-sharing only and items for discussion. It is surprising how strongly and frequently you may need to reiterate that some items are not for discussion, and providing a strong rationale ("Caddy has already done a lot of work on this and has used the views of a working group which includes some of you here, and we're happy with this direction for the moment") will be critical to not reopen old debates. Firmly but clearly refer anyone wishing to have a discussion to do so after the meeting, perhaps in your planned one-to-one or line management.

For meeting items requiring discussion and debate, it is sensible to orchestrate a way to ensure that everyone's voice is heard. With large teams, think-pair-share works surprisingly well, and I've even seen colleagues use mini-white boards to brilliant affect in large meetings to get a range of short ideas which colleagues can then be prompted to expand on further.

While soliciting views on how helpful (or not) and organised (or not) meetings are is enlightening, the greatest test of a meeting's effectiveness is the impact. Determine tangible outcomes – rather than "everyone is aligned on teaching quality," have

> when we watch a video clip of our new Maths teacher, all colleagues will have identified the following areas for development: need to be more responsive to in-lesson needs, to not talk when pupils are talking, and to review unit 5 with the Head of Department to check it is as good as it can be.

## SEND (special educational needs and disabilities): statutory duties

While the importance of the special educational needs co-ordinator (SENCO) in leading great teaching and a broad and balanced curriculum has been outlined in earlier chapters, there are some aspects of this role which are non-negotiable and statutory, and it is worth being aware of these as leaders.

In the SEND Code of Practice, there are four areas of need mapped out: (1) communication and interaction, (2) cognition and learning, (3) social, emotional and mental health, and (4) sensory and/or physical. These should be used by leaders as a support in identifying pupils who may have an additional need, with the proviso that few pupils fall neatly into a single category and pupils will often cut across these. Identifying pupils as requiring support in one of these areas does not automatically mean they require additional intervention work.

The Code of Practice advocates an "assess, plan, do, review" cycle whereby schools should approach pupils with potential SEND by assessing those needs, planning to address them, putting the plan into action, and reviewing its impact before re-assessing any changing or unmet needs. Pupils with an Education, Health and Care Plan (EHCP) must have this plan reviewed at least annually. The Code of Practice advocates regular assessment of pupils, as their needs can change over time, particularly (one hopes) with effective interventions which may "catch up" pupils and lead them to requiring something different in the future. This process should be undertaken with consultation of the pupil, parents, and teachers, and teachers must be informed of the plan. Parents can be especially helpful in supporting the plan if they can reinforce any strategies at home. These need to be reviewed following the system set out in the SEND Code of Practice and any Local Authority guidance.

In terms of the "plan" aspect, there is a definite lean towards "quality-first teaching" at the time of writing; that is, pupils' needs are to be met first and foremost within the mainstream classroom. Whether or not there are any additional interventions, the responsibility for the child's progress begins and ends with the teacher. Interventions such as specialist support from an educational psychologist or speech and language therapist will complement and not replace the classroom experience.

If you are managing the SEND aspect of your school, you will need to publish details about your school's approach in a SEND Information Report annually. Details of this are laid out clearly in the SEND code of practice.

The school SENCO must be a qualified teacher, ideally on the SLT, and within three years of being appointed, they will need to undertake the NPQ for SENCOs (previously the National Award in Special Educational Needs Co-ordination). It is their responsibility to check the EHCPs of any incoming pupils and determine whether the school can meet these pupils' needs. Through this process, it is important to support any SENCO, but particularly a SENCO who is new to post. If the school genuinely cannot meet the needs of the pupil, it is important that the school's response cite the EHCP itself and their own practice and then how meeting the needs of said pupil would not be conducive to either their own progress or the progress of other pupils. One SENCO I worked with used a three-column table for this, where the first column was a direct quotation from the EHCP, the middle would outline our school approach, and the righthand side would explain why this was or was not conducive to their or others' educational experience.

SENCOs will also be responsible for identifying and monitoring all pupils with SEND within your setting and need to have a clear and well-communicated process for this. There then must be a system for sharing this information with teachers and finally for checking they are following this guidance.

A SEND link governor can be a tremendous support in this work. Ensuring that they are properly trained and appropriately committed and having someone who can meet the SENCO regularly to check their thinking will be extremely beneficial for all.

## Safeguarding

Similarly, safeguarding is partly about training and communicating well with colleagues and partly about statutory obligations. Clearly, ensuring that all leaders have a strong understanding of the core safeguarding guidance "Keeping Children Safe in Education" is critical to ensure that they can lead understanding and application of this guidance with all school colleagues. Having your Designated Safeguarding Lead highlight changes to guidance annually as well as core information everyone could do with being reminded of will be important.

Having time to discuss the systems of safeguarding in school and check those systems is also important. You should have some sort of easy-to-use flow diagram or similar to log and follow up on concerns, and all members of staff should be clear on how to use this. If someone else holds records, ensure that you are checking these regularly by selecting a sample and doing a deep dive together. Of course, go about this in pursuit of a shared understanding of open safeguarding cases and the efficacy or otherwise of your system – it isn't so much an accountability check for that individual as a team accountability check for all your systems.

When concerns are raised over safeguarding, the Designated Safeguarding Lead (DSL) has three options. In order of seriousness these are to manage the case internally through the school's internal systems, to make an early help assessment, or to refer to social services. The latter two options involve liaising with external services, and so it is vital that both the DSL (who needs to be a member of the school's leadership team) and their deputy (an increasingly common appointment due to the level of administration involved) have ample time for their role. These calls are so time-sensitive they cannot find themselves on tomorrow's to-do list.

As schools need to keep records of every referral made and the subsequent action taken; many use online systems so individual pupil cases can be tracked with ease. This has the added benefit of seeing a series of seemingly minor concerns and deciding to escalate something that, on its own, may not seem overly serious. Where children have a social worker or are looked after or previously looked after, this should be known by the DSL and any relevant administrative and educational staff as it could inform adaptations to school approaches. For example, some looked-after children may be at risk of running away, and so if they are absent from school, their absence call may be made far sooner than for other pupils, and depending on the carer's response, the social worker may need to be looped in.

Policies are an important aspect of any role, but it is especially important that the safeguarding policy be accurate and up to date as well as that the behaviour policy, any online policy, and staff code of conduct incorporate relevant safeguarding aspects.

It is the responsibility of the DSL and ultimately the Headteacher (though I suppose everything is ultimately the Head's responsibility) to ensure that all staff adhere to safer recruitment practices. Most importantly, this is the opportunity for candidates to declare a criminal record upon applying, ensuring that interview questions assess candidates' suitability to work with children and thorough pre-employment checks, including verifying references, and ensuring that candidates provide a new, clear Disclosure and Barring Service (DBS) certificate.

All the staff information linked to safeguarding must be captured in the school's single central record. There are a number of statutory checks that need to be held here for all staff, and these are outlined in Keeping Children Safe in Education (the core safeguarding document for all colleagues). At the time of writing, this includes an identity check, enhanced DBS check, prohibition from teaching check, additional checks if the staff member has lived outside the UK, a check of their qualifications, and that they have the right to work in the UK (where required). Schools must maintain a similar record, though not so extensive, for governors, agency staff, volunteers, peripatetic music teachers, and contractors.

Schools must have robust processes for when visitors enter the school: they must sign in and out, and many schools will have them wear a lanyard so that all staff can be aware of whether they need to be accompanied. For example, visitors without a DBS will need to be accompanied at all times, and so having a red lanyard makes them particularly visible for staff to challenge if they are spotted alone on the site.

Managing allegations against staff is normally a responsibility held at Headteacher level, as it bridges the important realms of safeguarding and human resources (HR) in a way this level of seniority is appropriate to work at. If the head, with their training and experience to inform them, judges the allegation to meet the threshold of harm, they contact the Local Authority Designated Safeguarding Officer (LADO). Even if the head does not judge it to meet this threshold, in my experience the LADO is incredibly willing to support the judgement call they make and give advice on how to handle the allegation.

Keeping Children Safe in Education details what to do following an allegation, stipulating that leaders must remember their duty of care to both the child and the staff member throughout what is almost always a stressful and upsetting situation for all involved.

The head will usually want to conduct an investigation into almost any allegation, and they will usually ask a member of SLT to do this. They will be required to make a judgement on the findings, and so it is improper for them to conduct the investigation they will eventually rule on.

If you are tasked to conduct such an investigation, it can be one of the most challenging aspects of leadership to manage. You are investigating your colleagues and sometimes peers you know well. You have to keep an open mind and remember that we will never know everything about even those closest to us. When interviewing colleagues, retain the utmost compassion – often, a lack of judgement is not correlated to a wish to cause harm, and many will feel devastated about their mistake and fearful for their livelihood. Proceed with empathy and kindness. You may need to acquire pupil statements; if so, collect from a range and not just those who are friends with the child who made the allegation. Seek advice from the Head of Year on friendship groups if you are unsure.

## Working with a multi academy trust

I've worked as a senior leader in one Local Authority school, one stand-alone academy, one small MAT, and one large MAT, and largely I'd say that in my experience this has not been the decisive factor in the difference between leading these schools. The only experience that is different from the others is the large MAT experience, and that is because with a large MAT there are central services – people doing very specific jobs across all the schools – as well as greater consistency between schools in everything from policies to teaching practices to curriculum.

Undoubtedly, headship within a MAT is an easier job. Unlike the stand-alone head, you have a ready-made peer group that, at least in some MATs, you're given time to be with outside of school. This is incredibly supportive to making headship a more collegiate and, in my experience, enjoyable position. You are also given excellent support in the key functions that heads are expected to hold – things like HR, operations, and finance tend to be held at central level, reducing the pressure on heads to suddenly become experts in the things they've not yet encountered before taking on the role.

For senior leaders, being part of a MAT has positives and negatives. The amount of autonomy I've enjoyed at SLT level is not always afforded to those working to consistency across schools, and the role can become more about implementation than exploring new ideas – no bad thing when it comes to supportive school improvement but not always the thing that leaders are most excited by. Much like the centralised curriculum that reduces teacher workload but also curtails their creativity, the same is true of leadership in a medium-sized or larger MAT – the job is easier but perhaps less fun.

Central services can be both a great support and an irritation to leaders. Some functions will have a strong sense of what schools are like and understand the demands on leaders' time; some will not. It is important to feed back to your head where central teams are making unusual or inappropriate asks of leaders' time.

There is often a tension between those working in schools and those working in central teams. There is, from school colleagues, the sense that those in the central team have easier lives than those in schools. From central teams, there is the reluctant recognition that this is probably true, coupled with the reality that people working within the school system, no matter what their workplace, are working very hard and not being paid very well compared with their peers in other industries. Those in central teams are working to make schools better and certainly do not aspire to make colleagues' lives harder.

Where central services aren't working as well as they might, try to give feedback in the same way you would a school colleague. It is too easy to complain or take your frustrations out on people you rarely see and who turn up to work at 9 a.m. when you've already worked two solid hours at the coal face. Retain a feeling of positivity in your interactions and remain solutions-focused – don't just tell them all the ways they're failing you; suggest a way that would work better. Suggesting a new, more school-friendly way of dealing with common issues will be immensely valuable to central teams.

When thinking about improving your school, always look to the higher-performing schools in your trust. It is too tempting for colleagues to write off better results as "they have a better staff team" or "an easier intake." These sister schools are a great resource for you to make improvements in your context. I'd aim to visit every school doing better than yours that time allows for and retain the lens: what can I learn from this that will improve my school? Unlike high-performing schools not in your trust, those within your MAT have a link to you and will be a connection you can draw on and troubleshoot with over time.

MATs also provide a ready-made support network for all levels of leadership – all the SENCOs, DSLs, leaders responsible for teaching, and so on can link up together and share practice.

Finally, sometimes you are looking for something from a MAT central team and it is not forthcoming. If you ever ask a central team member for something, just as you would an in-school colleague, set a reminder to follow up in a week's time. Central teams are often working to very different timescales and deadlines to schools, and some will allow team members to take annual leave during the school term. This can mean that things are missed or not prioritised in the way you would expect. Retain an assumption of good will, and copy in those senior to the individual only after you've made an ask and sent one chase, unless it is deeply urgent – in which case, recognise you're asking for something with a very tight turnaround.

## Key takeaways

- Invest time and energy in making the trains run on time – none of the important stuff of learning happens without this.

- Train teachers to do duty with the seriousness and attention to detail you would any other training.

- Ensure that you invest time in working with and developing non-teaching colleagues.

## Notes

1 https://teachlikeachampion.org/tag/be-seen-looking-radar-what-to-do/ "Pastore's Perch" is a term used by educators to indicate being in a position where you have maximum sight-lines of the pupils, as displayed by Doug Lemov in this blog.
2 https://teachlikeachampion.org/tag/be-seen-looking-radar-what-to-do/ "Pastore's Perch" is a term used by educators to indicate being in a position where you have maximum sight-lines of the pupils, as displayed by Doug Lemov in this blog.
3 https://www.gov.uk/guidance/integrated-curriculum-and-financial-planning-icfp.

# 5 Finally

## What about vision?

I'd originally not planned to include anything about vision in this book, having written about it already in my previous book, *Culture Rules*. I've been increasingly wary of generic leadership practices: indeed, Viviane Robinson's work has thoroughly explored the comparison between the more generic leadership style known as "transformational" and domain-specific, education-based leadership – or "instructional leadership" – and has found that "the effect of instructional leadership on student outcomes was three to four times as great as that of transformational leadership."[1] Ultimately, what matters most is the way that leaders can implement their strong, evidence-based knowledge of school-specific practices.

That said, I'd like to add a short post-script about the practical aspects of vision, particularly around how to get a community on board. Moreover, the best leaders I've encountered have been so driven by what they want to achieve for pupils that it has seemed second nature for them to draw on these ideas and language in any conversation. It makes their decision making much easier because they see all decisions through this lens: "will this level the playing field for our pupils?," for example.

School visions are normally rather similar. Most leaders seek for some combination of academic excellence, future flourishing, access to opportunities, and citizenship from young people. Occasionally, there will be some maverick extras thrown in which reflect a particular community or a particular interest of the leader, but I have yet to see a school vision I couldn't get on board with, largely because all schools want to do the same thing. There isn't a school that longs for young people to do poorly academically and have limited choices. I've not yet, as it happens, met a pupil who wants to do poorly or a parent who wishes for their offspring to leave school without access to future employment. I've also not met any hard-working teachers who believe their pupils are all destined for failure.

So the vision itself is rarely the problem. The problem comes when the vision doesn't match the behaviours and actions of teachers, pupils, or parents. Pupils can say they want to do well and can also disrupt every lesson. Parents can say they want their child to do well and can also refuse for them to attend after-school

DOI: 10.4324/9781003465461-6

interventions to support their learning or detentions that will support their developing stronger habits of behaviour. Teachers can say they want their children to do well and can also plan lessons that don't stretch the children. Some teachers I've worked with have a general belief in pupils' potential but, when pushed to think about *particular* children or *particular* classes, will admit defeat. "Oh, but they're in year 10 – and they're so far behind, they will never catch up." "That class are just difficult. They'll never behave."

It doesn't matter which group we start with, but because we probably have more ability to influence teachers, we'll start there.

Telling teachers the school vision is not the start and end of the process. We have to get teachers on board and thinking on a specific class and child level. Leaders have to be brave to challenge low expectations, which will rarely present themselves overtly unless speaking about a particularly challenging case. Asking individual teachers when you work with them: "What do you want for Billy? How can we transform Shevonnae's future?" will be much more effective in getting teachers to think more positively about their ability to influence the young people in their care. We have to get teachers to think about their most challenging pupils in a positive and solutions-focused way. That can be through a structured, whole-school session or through one-to-one conversations. As leaders, our role is to know the classes who are underachieving, or, even better, the individual pupils who could be doing more, and talk to teachers about those individual, particular kids. Listen to what they say, and if you sense any low expectations coming through, gently rebut these and start to challenge their way of thinking.

In terms of securing buy-in from pupils, setting aside a few assemblies to let them know the sky is the limit won't normally be that effective. By all means, use your assembly slots to indoctrinate pupils with messages of positivity and an ethos of effort – what I'd call "benign brainwashing" – but it cannot end there. What pupils require to believe in such messages is to feel successful. Pupils are motivated by success, so schools have to put in the work to make pupils first feel, and then be, successful.

This is largely a question of curriculum pitch and pedagogy. If teachers are starting from where their children are and pitching frequent low-stakes assessment so they can ace it, that will build their motivation. Rosenshine advocates aiming for an 80% success rate: above this and children aren't learning, below this and they feel the gap is unbridgeable. With only 20% left to learn or improve, pupils can get stuck into feeling like they're at the final hurdle each lesson.

In terms of pupil behaviour, you must relentlessly raise expectations and expect them to reach them. Where pupils fall short of expectations, rely on both sanctions and education to redress this. Make use of whole-class or year-group resets. If one year 8 class is repeatedly getting it wrong, for example, repurpose their tutor time for a couple of weeks, put your best Senior Leadership Team, Head of Year, or most loved teacher in with them, and have them lead students through the routines while explaining again and again how these will link to improved learning.

Parents in secondary schools can feel far removed from what is going on, so leaders need to seize every communication opportunity to reiterate what you believe. Link every uniform or attendance reminder to your vision for pupil success. Begin every parent meeting by letting them know what the school stands for and how this will help their particular child.

But again, success is the only real convincing aspect for parents. Get the children succeeding, then invite parents in to see it. First, fix your school so you're proud of the lessons and everything in between, then allow parents to see it in all its glory. Ultimately, parents lose trust when institutions appear to be failing their child, either by not teaching them effectively or by excluding them from learning – and by exclusion, I mean the full gamut from pupils standing outside the classroom to a formal suspension.

The work of embedding a vision and ensuring that your entire school community shares it is particularly challenging because ultimately this work rests on conducting, completing, and revealing the entire work of school improvement.

## Note

1 Robinson, V. M. J., Lloyd, C., & Rowe, K. J. (2008). The impact of leadership on student outcomes: An analysis of the differential effects of leadership type. *Educational Administration Quarterly*, 44(5), 635–674.

# Bibliography

Paul Bambrick-Santoyo: *Leverage Leadership* Jossey Bass 2012.

Department for Education: "Guidance: Integrated Curriculum and Financial Planning" available at https://www.gov.uk/guidance/integrated-curriculum-and-financial-planning-icfp (accessed 28 March 2024).

Education Endowment Foundation: Effective Professional Development: Guidance Report 2021.

Education Endowment Foundation: Putting Evidence to Work: A school's Guide to Implementation 2019.

Education Endowment Foundation: The DNA of Reading Comprehension available at https://educationendowmentfoundation.org.uk/news/eef-blog-the-dna-of-reading-comprehension-knowledge-skills-and-strategies (accessed 23 September 2023).

Education Endowment Foundation: Special Educational Needs in Mainstream Schools available at https://d2tic4wvo1iusb.cloudfront.net/production/eef-guidance-reports/send/EEF_Special_Educational_Needs_in_Mainstream_Schools_Guidance_Report.pdf?v=1695537818 (accessed 24 September 2023).

John Hattie: *Visible Learning: The Sequel* Routledge 2023.

E.D. Hirsch: *Cultural Literacy* Vintage 1988.

E.D. Hirsch: *Why Knowledge Matters* Harvard Education Press 2016.

Doug Lemov: *Teach Like a Champion 3*.0 Jossey-Bass 2021.

Peps McCrea: *Developing Expert Teaching* 2023.

Robert Pondiscio: *How the Other Half Learns* Avery 2019.

V. M. J. Robinson, C. Lloyd, K. J. Rowe: The Impact of Leadership on Student Outcomes: An Analysis of the Differential Effects of Leadership Type. *Educational Administration Quarterly*, 44(5), 635–674, 2008.

Barak Rosenshine: "Principles of Instruction" American Educator 2012. available at: https://www.aft.org/sites/default/files/Rosenshine.pdf (accessed 17 January 2024).

S. Sims, H. Fletcher-Wood, A. O'Mara-Eves, S. Cottingham, C. Stansfield, J. Van Herwegen, J. Anders: *What are the Characteristics of Teacher Professional Development that Increase Pupil Achievement? A Systematic Review and Meta-Analysis* Education Endowment Foundation 2021.

S. Sims, H. Fletcher-Wood, A. O'Mara-Eves, S. Cottingham, C. Stansfield, J. Goodrich, J. Van Herwegen, J. Anders: Effective teacher professional development: new theory and a meta-analytic test. (EdWorkingPaper: 22-507) 2022. Retrieved from Annenberg Institute at Brown University: https://doi.org/10.26300/rzet-bf74 (accessed 28 March 2024)

Sam Strickland: *The Behaviour Manual* John Catt 2022.

Charlie Taylor's Behaviour Checklist: available at https://www.wigan.gov.uk/Docs/PDF/Resident/Education/Educational-Support/TESS/Charlie-Taylor-checklist.pdf (accessed 28 March 2024)

Dylan Wiliam: *Embedded Formative Assessment* Solution Tree Press 2011.

# Index

Printed in the United States
by Baker & Taylor Publisher Services